"Jenna Riemersma is a gifted couns
municator. This book will challenge, inform, and encourage,
courageous journey to know yourself and more deeply experience the love
of God. It is practical, accessible, and profound, and will help you love yourself and your neighbor more authentically and wholly than ever before."

—ROB GIBSON, PSAP; executive director,
The Cross Ministry Group, Denver, Colorado

"Jenna Riemersma helps readers experience both self-compassion and
God's grace through the revolutionary perspective of Internal Family
Systems therapy. This instructive guide is a must-read for individuals
struggling with addiction, trauma, mental illness, or internalized shame.
Jenna's charming personal stories are intertwined with scripture to make
this book both engaging and enlightening."

—STEFANIE CARNES, PhD; president, International Institute of Trauma
and Addiction Professionals, Wickenburg, Arizona; clinical architect,
Willow House at The Meadows, Carefree, Arizona; author of
Courageous Love: A Guide for Couples Conquering Betrayal

"Jenna has given the evangelical church a great gift! She has taken Internal Family Systems (IFS) therapy and made it understandable to the
typical follower of Christ. Her gift of language and her lively sense of
humor invite us to enter into the profound truths of Internal Family Systems. This a must-read for anyone interested in bringing much-needed
healing to the body of Christ. Above all the book will help you to begin
to comprehend the complexity of your own soul. As a sexual addiction
counselor for over thirty years in the church, I have seen at close range
the devastation that takes place when we are not acquainted with our
own brokenness. And I have seen the IFS approach to be an incredibly
effective method in helping people find the healing they have sought,
sometimes for decades. The only problem I have with the book is that I
didn't write it. Jenna has done an exquisite job! *Altogether You* is the best
Christian book I have found on the subject."

—TED ROBERTS, DMin; best-selling author;
founder of Pure Desire Ministries International, Gresham, Oregon

"Too many Christians, including me, have been bound by shame regarding the parts of us that are 'bad'—the parts we desperately hide from others and hate in ourselves. Finally, we have a compassionate, Christian-based guide about what to do with our "firefighters" parts that are only trying to extinguish our pain. *Altogether You* folds the clinical richness of Internal Family Systems into the graceful truth of the gospel: all parts are welcome! With gentleness, humor, and readability, Jenna Riemersma shows us how to access the God Image within and allow the resulting transformation to lead us home. Hallelujah! Every Christian needs to read this book."

—Marnie C. Ferree, LMFT, CSAT; founder and director,
Bethesda Workshops, Nashville, Tennessee;
author of *No Stones: Women Redeemed from Sexual Addiction*

"*Altogether You* is a beautiful and practical commentary on God's love and his relational nature imprinted on every human. In this book I heard the gentle invitation to agree with God about *all* of the parts of me, not just some parts. Jenna Riemersma is an expert who writes like a friend as she brilliantly guides us on the journey of Self-leadership, moving toward a place where 'all parts are welcome.' This book will give you a theology and a psychology for both the ordinary and extraordinary circumstances of your life."

—Clifton Roth, PSAP; executive director
of CrossPoint Ministry, Louisville, Kentucky

"If you are struggling to make sense of yourself, if you feel like you don't know who you are, if you want to reclaim your true self, READ THIS BOOK! *Altogether You* is a book I will be recommending for my clients, and I highly recommend it to anybody who wants to understand who they really are."

—Dr. Kevin Skinner, PhD, LMFT; cofounder and clinical director,
Addo Recovery, Lindon, Utah; author of *Treating Trauma
from Sexual Betrayal*, *Treating Pornography Addiction*,
and *Treating Sexual Addiction*

"Psychological concepts and theological constructs unite in Jenna's readable, relatable book. Grounded in scripture, *Altogether You* is an accessible introduction to Richard Schwartz's Internal Family Systems theory for any Christian reader experiencing emotional pain. And for anyone holding on to the idea that you are somehow flawed or permanently broken, Jenna will expertly help you to gently let go and come home."

—KELLY MCDANIEL, LPC, NCC, CSAT,
Nashville, Tennessee; author of
Ready to Heal: Breaking Free of Addictive Relationships

"Jenna Riemersma has expert knowledge of Internal Family Systems theory. In *Altogether You,* she teaches it experientially like nobody else can—and more importantly, she lives it. She brings those resources together into a synergistic choreography that is both professionally and personally impactful."

—ADRIAN HICKMAN, PhD, LMFT, LPC; founder and CEO,
Capstone Treatment Center, Judsonia, Arkansas

"In this ingenious application of Dr. Richard Schwartz's transformative Internal Family Systems theory to Christianity, Jenna Riemersma illuminates how this secular psychotherapeutic model offers specific techniques to facilitate our connection with the Imago Dei that resides at our core. This allows us to unleash our innate capacity to hold a powerful, witnessing, and healing presence with the wounded and burdened parts of ourselves, as Jesus did with all those he encountered. In her informal, relatable style, and using scripture as a guide, Jenna insightfully distinguishes between authentic spirituality and the well-intentioned, though often misguided, counterproductive attempts of our spiritualizer parts to bring us closer to God. In this invitation to move toward and heal our pain, Jenna lays out a path that allows us to stop striving to get to 'God over there' and surrender to 'God in here.'"

—ALEXIA D. ROTHMAN, PhD; certified IFS therapist
and international IFS speaker/educator, Atlanta, Georgia

"Christians, take notice. Some have mistakenly thought there was a conflict in psychotherapy, psychology, and our faith. Jenna Riemersma has done a masterful job of helping the reader understand the power of Internal Family Systems by viewing it through the lens of scripture and faith. This should be the next book you read."

—MILTON S. MAGNESS, PhD, LPC, CSAT;
founder and director, Hope & Freedom Counseling Services,
Houston, Texas; author of *Thirty Days to Hope & Freedom from
Sexual Addiction*, *Stop Sex Addiction*, and *Real Hope, True Freedom*

"In her book, *Altogether You*, Jenna Riemersma has masterfully woven together Internal Family Systems therapy and numerous principles of spiritual transformation to forge an essential framework for better understanding who we are, why we do what we do, and what we need in order to flourish in life and in relationships. To anyone who wants to integrate their personal faith in Christ into the process of healing, growth, and personal discovery, this book is most certainly for you."

—TODD BOWMAN, PhD, LCPC, CSAT-C; director, SATP Institute,
Olathe, Kansas; associate professor of counseling,
Indiana Wesleyan University; author of *Angry Birds and Killer Bees:
Talking to Your Kids About Sex*; editor of *Reclaiming Sexual Wholeness*

"As I read *Altogether You*, I often reflected that the words *healing, whole,* and *holy* all come from the same Latin root meaning essentially to become complete and entire. Riemersma eloquently helps us understand how Christians become stuck in our incompleteness, but she also provides a map to return us to our natural state of living in communion, fully receiving the love and grace of God."

—CRAIG S. CASHWELL, PhD, LPC, NCC, ACS, CSAT-S;
professor in counselor education, The College of William & Mary,
Williamsburg, Virginia; coauthor, *Shadows of the Cross*
and *Clinical Mental Health Counseling*

ALTOGETHER
YOU

ALTOGETHER
YOU

Experiencing personal and
spiritual transformation with
Internal Family Systems therapy

JENNA RIEMERSMA, LPC

PIVOTAL PRESS
Marietta, GA

ALTOGETHER YOU:
*Experiencing personal and spiritual transformation
with Internal Family Systems therapy*

Copyright © 2020 by Jenna Riemersma

Pivotal Press
Marietta, Georgia

www.JennaRiemersma.com

Printed in the United States of America
First Edition 2020

ISBN 978-1-7349584-0-9 (softcover)
ISBN 978-1-7349584-1-6 (ebook)
Library of Congress Control Number: 2020907414

Cover design: Yvonne Parks, Pear Creative
Interior design and typeset: Katherine Lloyd, The DESK

CONTENTS

PART ONE: WHAT'S REALLY GOING ON
Learning why we are divided against ourselves

PART TWO: THIS CHANGES EVERYTHING
Transforming our relationships with ourselves, others & God

FOREWORD

Thirty years ago, I could never have imagined writing a foreword to a book like this. My father was a scientist who taught us that religion was at the root of many of the world's conflicts and slaughters. I maintained a skepticism about anything spiritual until I began exploring my clients' inner terrains and encountered their Self. The existence of this undamaged, healing essence—even in people who had been horribly abused and suffered terrible traumas early in life—could not be explained by the psychological theories I had studied.

Reading this book made my heart sing. With wit, raw self-disclosure, and engaging writing, Jenna translates my life's work for Christians. In the process, she illuminates many of the well-meaning but unhelpful ways that the Bible has been used to try to get people to behave, and no less based in scripture.

About twenty years ago I was invited to teach my approach, called Internal Family Systems Therapy (IFS), to students at the Reformed Theological Seminary in Jackson, Mississippi, which was and remains a strongly evangelical, conservative program. I went to Jackson with significant trepidation, and while it was difficult to find common ground on everything, at one point, one of the participants exclaimed excitedly, "Now I get it. You are helping people do inside themselves what Jesus did in the outside world: go to and love the exiled parts of us in the same way he loved the lepers, the poor, the outcasts!" It was a beautiful moment of mutual connection. They still teach Internal Family Systems Therapy at Reformed Theological Seminary.

After that experience I became much more interested in Jesus and how his teaching parallels IFS. So when I read this book, I was thrilled. Not only does Jenna highlight that parallel and many more, she fills the book with examples we can all relate to, and explains IFS in a simple and compelling way.

This is a groundbreaking and courageous book. It challenges Christians everywhere to reflect on ways in which their religious teaching may inadvertently lead them away from self-acceptance and love—away from the very principles that Jesus taught. The way in which you relate to your own parts will parallel how you relate to people who resemble those parts. If you hate or fear an angry part of yourself, for example, you will struggle to have compassion and forgiveness for an angry person in your life. As Jenna makes clear, trying to love others while shaming ourselves is not only futile, but also totally unnecessary. Jesus wants nothing more than for us to bring more love to both ourselves and to our relationships with others.

It is with great excitement that I invite you to explore the illuminating and life-giving truths in these pages. Welcome to a scripture-centered new way of love.

Dr. Richard Schwartz
Boston, Massachusetts

PREFACE

Have you ever felt that every part of who you are is truly welcome? Not just the you that does things right and is polite and feels positive feelings, but also the parts of you that mess up, say the wrong things, and feel lonely, afraid, and ashamed?

And by *welcome*, I don't mean that those difficult aspects of you are tolerated until you get your act together. No, I mean accepted, received, and valued—exactly as you are.

If you answered "yes" to that question, you are a rare and fortunate person. For most of us, the answer to that question is "no."

The truth is that in our families, communities, places of worship, schools, workplaces, and relationships, it's often not safe to be our authentic selves. We may not even be safe for ourselves *within* ourselves. When we mess up, say the wrong things, or feel difficult feelings, we may judge and shame and harshly criticize ourselves. We may believe God does that to us too.

Maybe this is why we love our dogs so much. Regardless of what we've done or how we feel, they are always happy to see us, waiting at the door when we come home. They don't judge us. They just want to love us. And isn't that what we all need more of?

The common experience of not feeling fully welcome and having to disown parts of ourselves brings untold suffering, hiding, and shame. It keeps our relationships shallow and drives our addictions and pain. It's the thing that happened (allegorically or factually, whatever you prefer) in Eden the moment things went south. When we felt exposed and ashamed, we started sewing fig leaves to hide from each other and from God. But it's hard to find fig leaves big enough to cover all the stuff we're ashamed of.

I spent much of my early life hiding behind leaves. I'm an only child who grew up in a military family, and doing things "perfectly" felt important to me. We moved so frequently I never quite knew where home was.

Thankfully, I had loving, caring parents. But life still delivers its share of pain and hurt, and when I didn't do it all perfectly, I started to hide the real me.

I tried to overperform my way into feeling okay. I tried staying so busy that none of those yucky feelings could get to the surface. I thought if I could keep people around me happy, I would always feel worthy and safe.

Not surprisingly, I became a therapist. My job as a therapist is to focus on other people's feelings and needs and make other people okay, so that was a pretty familiar role for me. Because I want to be a good therapist, I've done a lot of my own healing work. On that transformational journey I was introduced to the model of therapy that this book is based on: Internal Family Systems. And for the first time I had the *felt* experience that all parts of me were welcome. That I could drop my leaves. That I didn't have to achieve and perform and get all of the parts of me to "do it right" before I could be my authentic self without fear of judgment. I experienced the reality of grace.

That's when I realized that this secular therapy was actually helping me experience my Christian faith more effectively than sometimes even my faith community did. For me, the IFS model paralleled in surprising ways the gospel of hope and grace that I had been acquainted with in the well-loved pages of the Bible on my nightstand—the hope and grace that I had always longed for, but rarely actually experienced.

I wrote this book so that you could experience that same hope and grace. If you're tired of having to pretend and cover up, if you've tried to change and failed, if you are disillusioned with the faith of your childhood, your faith has stalled, or you're questioning faith entirely, this book is my gift to you.

I want you to know that in the pages of this book, you are safe, and you are welcome. All of you. Exactly as you are. Every part of you is welcome, not just *tolerated* until you get your act together and stop doing and feeling bad things. As Brennan Manning said,

> *"You are loved just as you are. Not as you should be.*
> *Because you're never going to be as you should be."*

Jenna Riemersma
The Atlanta Center for Relational Healing
Atlanta, Georgia

Part One

What's Really Going On

*Learning why we are
divided against ourselves*

1

WHY ARE WE SO STUCK?

*"What I want to do, I do not do,
but what I hate, I do."*

We are all *stuck*.

And we don't know how to *un*stick our *stuck*.

As a therapist, I see this reality every day. I get to sit with all types of courageous people as they share some version of the same complaint: "I'm doing (or feeling) stuff I don't want to be doing (or feeling)." This internal battle leaves them feeling defective and weak. They do things they don't want to do, feel things they don't want to feel, and can't figure out how to turn things around.

I so relate. My guess is you do too.

We want to lose weight, but we eat Oreos. A whole package. In one sitting.

We want to be fit, but we can't seem to walk through the door of the gym.

We want great sex with the person we love, but we keep going back to porn.

We want peace but can't stop *doing* long enough to be still.

We want relationship with our children but spend dinners staring at screens.

We want to nurture the inner life but neglect our personal spiritual practice.

We want to be generous but keep spending our way into debt.

We want to be respected and respectful, but we blow up and rage.

We want romance but can't get past our partner's faults.

We want to feel hope and motivation but can't find the energy to get out of bed.

We want meaningful friendships but anxiety and shame keep us walled off.

We want to be sober but can't resist "just one more" glass of wine . . .

Clearly, stuckness is part of the human condition. We all know what it's like to try to change only to fall back into an all-too-familiar pattern.

But there *is* hope, and we're actually a lot closer to answers than we think. In fact, a key to change is hiding in a word we already use to describe our struggle.

The word is *part*.

WHAT'S REALLY GOING ON IN ME?

The unexpected truth I've gathered from years of experience as a therapist is that everyone gets stuck for the same reason: *one part of us wants one thing while another part of us wants something else.*

In other words, our parts are at war.

In the pages ahead, I will help you understand why we're so divided against ourselves and each other, and what to do about it. My approach is based squarely on the work of Dr. Richard Schwartz, who created a model for therapy called Internal Family Systems (IFS). Schwartz was the first to describe people as comprised of a core self and many separate parts. To put it another way, he showed that we don't go through life as one, internally consistent personality—all one thing all the time. Instead, we are more like an alliance of different parts, all representing very distinct aspects of what we think of as "the real me."

Internal Family Systems (IFS): A model of therapy developed by Dr. Richard Schwartz that understands human beings to be comprised of a core Self (referred to in this book as *God Image* or *Imago Dei*) and many different parts.

Now, that might sound a bit strange at first. But it isn't. I promise in just a few pages it will start to make sense.

Interestingly, therapists are applying Schwartz's insights to issues as wide ranging as PTSD, recovery from addiction and anxiety disorders, leadership, couples therapy, suicide prevention, and global conflicts. And to the point of this book, I have been delighted to discover that the IFS model deeply complements biblical insights and gives us tools to live out an authentic, Christ-honoring spirituality. If you're a person of faith, I'm confident you'll discover the same.

That is, if the word *parts* doesn't freak you out too much.

A part is just an aspect of you. A subpersonality, if you will.

Parts: Unique aspects of our personalities (subpersonalities) that have their own thoughts, feelings, sensations, and agendas. All people are born with many unburdened parts that together comprise their unique personality. All parts want something positive for the individual. Some parts become burdened with pain (or strategies for coping with pain) from negative life experiences.

It's helpful to remember that major figures in scripture describe an inner world of parts in conflict. Consider the Apostle Paul. He famously wrote: "I do not understand what I do. For what I want to do I do not do, but what I hate I do" (Romans 7:15). (Unless otherwise noted, all scripture quotations are from the NIV.) Consider David. He shares his Battle of the Parts all through the Psalms. One day it's, "I *absolutely* trust you God!" The next it's, "I'm dying here! Where are you, God?" And consider the Apostle James. He seems to point to the same dynamic when he asks, "What causes fights and quarrels among you? Don't they come from your desires that battle within you?" (James 4:1).

In the centuries since, Augustine, Luther, and countless other Christian thinkers have chronicled the battles of their parts. These confessions along with some key recent findings in the human sciences give me hope that being stuck doesn't need to be the end of the story.

For now, if the word *part* feels uncomfortable, replace it with a word like *component, aspect,* or *subpersonality.* The important insight is not what we call it, but the ability to realize that *when I'm feeling or doing something I don't want to feel or do, I'm not a bad person, I simply have parts at war.*

With that small shift, behaviors and feelings most of us have struggled helplessly with for years finally begin to make sense. If you're like me and thousands of others, you'll find that you can love yourself, others, and God in practical, often profound new ways. Your intimate relationships will mend and flourish. You'll find helpful insights on common emotional struggles—from depression, anxiety, and overeating to addiction and infidelity. Even how you understand and relate to other cultures and political parties will shift radically.

If you're skeptical, that's good! I hope you are so skeptical that you apply what you discover here . . . and actually *experience* the change.

FINDING OUR STUCKNESS

Your own stuckness may have come immediately to mind, or you might have a hard time connecting with the places in your life where you have parts at war. Our struggles are sometimes so familiar that they operate outside of our conscious awareness.

Following are some common places that people get stuck. Which ones resonate with you? Meditate on your response for a moment. How has this stuck place impacted you? Be courageous and honest. No judgment. No shame. Just a safe place to speak your truth.

Feelings

- Anxiety
- Depression
- Fear
- Worry
- Panic
- Despair/hopelessness
- Loneliness
- Isolation
- Shame
- Self-hatred

- Anger at God
- Spiritual crisis
- Bitterness/resentment
- Pride/arrogance
- Spiritual emptiness
- Spiritual stuckness
- Greed/entitlement
- Jealousy/envy

Thought and Behavior Patterns

- Negative self-talk
- Overeating/comfort eating
- Undereating/restricting/repeat dieting
- Overworking/compulsive busyness
- Underworking/laziness/underemployment
- Overspending/debt
- Hoarding/oversaving/miserliness
- Obsessive thoughts
- Compulsive behavior
- Underexercising/sloth
- Overexercising
- Oversleeping
- Undersleeping/insomnia
- Drinking for relief or to drunkenness
- Drugging
- Sexual acting out (porn, affairs, etc.)
- Sexual acting in (avoidance, comparison, etc.)
- Dissociating/checking out/binge watching
- Avoidance/isolating
- Denial
- Procrastination

Relationship Patterns

- Anger/rage/outbursts of temper
- Staying in toxic relationships

- Sabotaging important relationships
- Making excuses
- Blame
- Lying/covering up/distortion
- Rescuing others
- People pleasing

If you're like me, you might have some checks on that list that you don't mind writing down, and others you wouldn't want anyone to see. The gift of speaking our truth is that we begin to see ourselves right where we are, stuckness and all, and that is the starting point for change.

KNOWING MORE
& OTHER UNHELPFUL SOLUTIONS

Sometimes we think: *If I just knew more, I could improve.* This assumes we have an information problem. But is that true? We know we should spend less money than we make. We know we should invest quality and quantity time with our children. We know we shouldn't have affairs. We move from one self-help podcast to another searching for the most expert insight possible.

> Knowing more doesn't make us behave differently.

But knowing more doesn't make us behave differently.

Most of us would have to agree with Paul. We know perfectly well the good we want to do, but we can't seem to always make ourselves do it. And if knowing more is rarely enough, neither are many other simplistic fixes.

Like this time-honored dictum: *Just stop it!*

Stop eating sugar.

Stop feeling anxiety.

Stop using porn.

When just stopping doesn't happen, the next alternative is often: *Try harder!* This one makes so much sense. "If you would just try harder (only eat grapefruit, pray better, resist the laptop), you wouldn't be so messed up."

We do try harder. And when change still doesn't happen, we suffer terribly from the rest of the message: "*If you don't stop it . . . you must be a failure. And if we see you can't stop it, we'll judge and shame you.*"

Shame on you for being fat (and for every woman on the planet, "fat" is defined as her current size). Shame on you for drinking. For letting your marriage falling apart. For being depressed. Or anxious. Or suicidal.

We even shame people for things that are not under their control: Shame on you for your spouse's sexual addiction. Or, shame on you for your kid's rebellion.

Inevitably, the *Shame on you* message morphs into the more lethal version we lay on ourselves, *Shame on me.*

Shame on me for being fat, being depressed, having a failed relationship, being in debt, drinking too much, not praying enough.

Sound painfully familiar?

The thing is, every one of these "answers" seem so right and true and altogether obvious. We really *should* be able to "just stop it," right? And trying harder *should* work. And, for crying out loud, laying on the shame and guilt is so excruciating it just *has* to make us change.

Actually, some of the time "learn more," "stop it," and "try harder" *do* work. For a while. That's what makes them so appealing. But if that's as far as we go, they eventually stop working. Because we've only addressed the symptom and not the cause. Which is why New Year's resolutions are typically completely shot by January 10, and the regulars at the gym can get space in the free weights again.

For many people of faith, these defeats feel even more crushing because they seem to fly in the face of the victory that scripture and church culture promise.

PRAYING AWAY THE BAD STUFF

In a perfect world, faith communities would be the safest places on earth for us to be honest about our universal human stuckness. Thankfully, they often are. But sometimes we find ourselves tempted to bring our unhelpful human "fixes" into our faith communities, and when we do, churches become the last places on the planet where we can be real about our struggles and our pain.

Unfortunately, communities of faith sometimes add to the problem when they simply spiritualize the same old fixes. I'll show you what I mean.

The spiritual version of "have more knowledge" tells me if I spend more time reading or memorizing the Bible, I won't have my struggle.

The spiritual version of "stop it" tells me to *Repent!* And nail my sin to the cross.

The spiritual version of "try harder" tells me to pray more. Confess more. Surrender more. Repeat these scriptures. Tape them on the mirror.

Different faith traditions might use different language. But the implied and sometimes stated promise is likely to be the same: If you just become more spiritually minded, you won't feel those negative feelings or do that bad stuff. You'll stop struggling.

Now, none of these spiritual responses are bad things. They are good, often powerful things. The problem comes when we try to force a spiritual solution without first asking or caring about the whys. *Why am I depressed? Why am I anxious? Why do I drink too much? Why am I over- or undereating? Why do my relationships keep faltering?*

If we don't know why we have those feelings or act in those ways, we'll have no idea how to address what's really going on, or what it is we really need God to heal. We will simply align with the part of us that doesn't want to feel or do those things, against the part that does. And war breaks out inside.

It only gets worse when we believe that all those "bad" things that "bad" parts of us do or feel just need to be gotten rid of, crushed by sheer will power, or eliminated, *before* we qualify as a good person of faith. Because sometimes we have this crazy expectation that if we are really living as Christians should, we won't do or feel any of that bad stuff.

I believe this breaks the heart of God. Scripture reveals a God who encourages us to cry out to him,[1] and "wrestle with him through the night."[2] Israel's most anguished poet, David, is also described in scripture as a man after God's own heart.[3]

I think God says to our hurt and pain and messy process: "Bring it, child. Bring it. I am right here with you in it."

COUSIN MYRTLE'S SICK CAT

I lived most of my life in this stuck dilemma. I grew up in church, invited God to take the helm of my life in my early twenties, and earnestly poured myself into learning everything I could about my faith. I have academic and striving parts of me that love to learn and "do it right." These parts of me did well in traditional Bible studies and church environments where I read the passage and gave the "right" answer and asked for prayer for my cousin Myrtle's sick cat.

I gained a lot of head knowledge about God and knew a lot of good and right answers. I was very well intentioned and did a lot of "right" stuff, too, so that helped me feel good about my journey. I taught stuff. I Vacation Bible Schooled. I mission tripped. I even cooked stuff for sick people, although I'm not a very good cook and my casseroles probably made them sicker.

That was all well and good until I lived long enough to walk through some difficult experiences—the kind of stuff you don't feel comfortable bringing up for prayer in a small group of nice, smiling people who all seem to have their act together. I had to stick to my cousin Myrtle's sick cat at prayer time and keep my truth hidden in my own secret darkness, because I didn't want to be shamed or judged by any spiritual version of "stop it" or "try harder."

I had moments of wishing I could have a health struggle instead of my actual struggles, because at least if I were in the hospital, I could be on the prayer chain and people would bring my family casseroles.

Let me say it a different way.

I wished I had cancer so I could be honest at church.

I couldn't be authentic, and that wore me out. I didn't throw out my faith. My heart still longed for relationship with God. But at pivotal junctures like these, many people do throw out their faith. Or they slap on the "plastic fantastic" mask of inauthentic living. With church attendance declining[4] rapidly, I suspect this happens a lot more than we'd like to admit.

Life will be difficult. We are not made perfect this side of heaven. We will always have stuff. Hard stuff. Stuff done to us, stuff we experience, and stuff we struggle with ourselves.

That's a promise from Jesus himself.[5] But if instead we fall into the distorted thinking that, *If I'm doing my faith right, then I won't have real struggles*, we have to hide behind the mask of spiritual perfectionism. There's no other choice if that's what we believe. Then we become very careful in our relationships that we don't let our "crazy" show. We stick to sharing about Myrtle's sick cat—and we slowly die inside because we can't be real.

> I discovered a completely new way of relating to stuckness that beautifully complemented my deep spiritual beliefs.

Mercifully, as he has many times in my faith journey, God showed me a way to connect with him that bypassed this guardedness. Within the model of Internal Family Systems, I discovered a completely new way of relating to stuckness that beautifully complemented my deep spiritual beliefs. It was practical, and immediately made a difference in the way I related to myself and others. It helped me get past judgment, shame, and despair, and begin to live in compassion, respect, and grace. It reintroduced me to a bigger, better God—the one I had never quite stopped hoping for.

I like to think it helped me be Jesus to all the inside parts of me, and to the people outside of me as well.

MY WAYS ARE NOT YOUR WAYS

Doing the opposite of what we think we should do (and feel) is a theme with God, who promises that his ways are not our ways. After all, when Jesus showed up in the world, he turned everyone's concept of God upside down. He challenged expectations of what a healthy spiritual and emotional life looked like and how it should behave—and having it all together at all times was definitely *not* it. He enjoyed hanging out with the least promising people and saved his hardest words for the shiny Guardians of Spiritual Awesomeness who thought they did and said all the right things. The ones who were experts in "stop it" and "try harder."

To show a new picture of what God was *really* like, Jesus preferred hanging out with ordinary folks. He moved toward the misbehaving, broken, suspect, messy-but-honest crowd. As you probably know, that crowd was where he went looking for his closest friends and followers.

To show more of God, Jesus also told stories. About a shepherd who went looking for his one silly, straying sheep. A father who ran toward his biggest-loser-of-all-time son.

That's what receiving the truth about who we are inside can do for us. It can show us that all our parts are welcome, that healing is possible, and that alive and well at our center is a powerful, transformative, God-created core—our God Image.

YOU'RE INVITED

Let's explore together the key concepts of this new way of living. I will share my own stories, support important insights with scripture and other sources, and lead you into the personal application necessary for you to experience change.

This book is for everyone who has struggled to make sense of the battle within.

For those of us who do things we don't want to do, and then wish we hadn't done. (Seriously, the Oreos were sitting there *staring* at me.)

For all of us who have tough questions about faith and are afraid to be honest.

For those of us who believe one way but live another.

For those of us who do feel afraid, lonely, anxious, resentful, vulnerable, or depressed. And then feel ashamed because those feelings don't seem okay for a "person of faith."

By the end of this book, you will have the opportunity to realize for yourself the kind of healing that eludes most people for years.

Welcome. I hope you feel right at home. You are not alone, and you don't have to stay stuck. You are human. And *all* parts of you are welcome.

Discussion Questions

- In what areas of your life do you wrestle with stuckness?

- When part of you wants to do one thing and a different part wants to do something else, that's a sign that your parts are at war. (Sleeping in vs. spending time with God. Eating Oreos vs. losing weight.) How do you typically respond when you have parts that seem to be at war?

- Have you ever felt afraid to be honest about your struggles? What qualities in a person or environment make it safe to be honest about the tough stuff?

- Have you ever heard "learn more," "stop it," or "try harder" in a spiritual context? How did these messages impact you?

- Are you prepared for God to turn your human way of thinking on its head? What excites you about that possibility?

THE WHOLE IS GREATER

How understanding our parts
changes how we change

If all this parts language is making you wonder if you have multiple personalities, the answer is . . . well . . . yes. You do. We all do. It's completely normal to have very different sides or aspects of our personalities that go together to make up our whole.

We intuitively understand this, and it shows in the way we talk.

"Hey Rachael, thanks for the invite to the party on Friday! Part of me really wants to go, but it's been such a long week at work that part of me wants to go home and crash early. Do you mind if I stop by for just an hour?"

Sometimes our hidden "war of parts" is relatively simple, like how we feel about the party on Friday. Other times its more serious or upsetting, like how we engage with an addiction or an ongoing battle with anxiety or depression. But no matter where our warring parts fall on that continuum, IFS insights about our parts and our core self can help.

We've seen how traditional attempts to reconcile our parts can leave us feeling shamed, judged, and unworthy. People of faith wonder if we are in sin or a disappointment to God. That's because neither "just stop" eating doughnuts nor "get more" spiritual discipline tend to work for very long.

In this chapter, we look at ideas of the self, get to know our parts, and figure out how to get from where we are to where we want to be. First, let me tell you the fascinating story of how this way of understanding ourselves came about.

OUT OF MANY, ONE

In the 1980s, Dr. Richard Schwartz was a young therapist in Chicago who had been trained in a model known as Family Systems. The model teaches that individuals are shaped by the complex web of primary relationships in their world. To make progress with a person's struggles required working with other members in the larger ecosystem. Family Systems helps us understand, for example, that if you have a teen who is drinking and also being verbally abused by his father, you have to treat the father's verbal abuse, the mother's avoidance, *and* the teen's drinking if you want to alleviate the problem; you can't treat symptoms or people in isolation.

But this approach has limits. Therapists found that even when issues within the family were addressed, symptoms often persisted. It was at this point that Schwartz made some remarkable breakthroughs.

He realized that systems or key relationships existed not only *outside* of clients (parents, uncles, competitive siblings, nasty neighbors), but *inside* of them as well. And those *internal systems* needed healing too.

Specifically, Schwartz noticed that his clients regularly described their suffering as resulting from different parts of themselves that were in horrible conflict. A client struggling with an eating disorder described a part of her that wanted to restrict food so she could be thin, in control, and gain approval, while another part of her wanted desperately to eat because she was starving and concerned about her health. These two parts were at war—literally—and the outcome of that war would determine whether the client lived or died.

Curious, Schwartz checked to see if other clients had these same kinds of parts in conflict. Sure enough, they did. When he drew his attention inside himself, he had to admit that he saw the same battlefield. That was how Internal Family Systems (IFS) as a therapeutic model was born.

At the time, people who were identified as having "parts" were viewed with a lot of skepticism. The diagnosis of Multiple Personality Disorder (now called Dissociative Identity Disorder) was considered either fictitious, bizarre, or highly pathological.

Showing considerable courage, Dick stepped into the psychological arena and gently suggested to his peers, *Um, guys, I think we all have these parts. Parts may be normal.*

You can imagine about how well that went over.

But Schwartz persisted. He wanted to know more about those warring parts: why they were doing what they were doing, and what prevented them from stopping. Turns out the best way to get answers was to ask the parts about themselves. When he tried that, he discovered they would respond. Not literally, like speaking in audible voices, but through images, memories, or the impression of thoughts. Not things that clients were manufacturing, either, or what the clients *thought* these parts would say, but actual interaction with the parts themselves.

What's more, he found that the parts were really happy that someone had finally noticed them and wanted to hear from them! (Honestly, you should read that sentence again.)

It was at this point that the fuller picture emerged.

Turns out that our parts have unique identities.

They have distinct personalities.

They have jobs that they are doing, burdens that keep them stuck in unhelpful ways of behaving, and ways they can be healed and freed up to do more helpful things.

These are the building blocks of the Internal Family Systems model. Schwartz was certainly not the first to become aware of our divided internal "family." But he was the first to create a practical and comprehensive approach to therapy out of that awareness.

And although IFS is a secular model, it nevertheless reflects deep scriptural truths about our humanity, beginning with how it understands our essential identity.

That's what I want to talk about next.

THE GOD IMAGE: OUR CORE

In his work, Schwartz observed a deep and stable essence within every human being. Schwartz called this essence the Self. Every person has a

Self. It is the core of a person that makes us who we are and is best equipped to lead our internal parts on a healing path.

Schwartz also saw that this Self was inherently good, wise, courageous, compassionate, joyful, and calm. Further, he realized that this one insight—that the core self is good—had huge implications. "Take a few minutes," he asks, "to imagine how your life would be different if you had more access to those qualities on a daily basis and trusted that this calm joyful Self was your true identity."[6]

At first blush, his view of the Self can seem to be at odds with what we hear in church, where the word *self* is usually correlated with negative, sinful, or narcissistic values. But I believe what Schwartz titled the "Self" is actually the fingerprint of God—the *Imago Dei* in every human being. The creation story describes this essence of who we as humans are as the Image of God. That is why in this book we'll mostly use the term *God Image* in place of the term *Self*.[7]

This God Image at our core is the seat of our authentic spirituality, and a reflection of the divine within us. As a pure and undamaged reflection of the qualities of God, it is where wisdom, connection, and compassion reside. When Genesis 1:27 tells us "God created mankind in his own image, in the image of God he created them; male and female he created them," it was a way of describing this essence. Our God-created core is always within us, even when we aren't in touch with it, and even if we don't believe it's there.

When we have full access to our God Image, we will spontaneously (with no effort) experience what Schwartz calls the Eight Cs: curiosity, compassion, courage, connection, clarity, calm, confidence, and creativity. In Galatians 5, scripture refers to these qualities as the fruit of the Spirit: love, joy, peace, patience, kindness, goodness, faithfulness, gentleness, and self-control. Whatever we call it, when we are fully connected to the God Image within, we are attuned to the presence and nature of God, and better resourced to move toward healing.

Every person has a God Image at their core, and in a perfect world it is surrounded by many unhindered parts that together make up our unique personalities.

Self (God Image or Imago Dei): Our central core that is who we truly are. The Self is the seat of our authentic spiritual connection to the divine. This book primarily uses the term *God Image*, or *Imago Dei*, to refer to Self, which reflects the Christian understanding that humans are made in the image of God (Genesis 1:27). The God Image is undamaged in all people and reflects qualities of the divine such as the fruit of the Spirit or the Eight C qualities. The goal of IFS therapy, and of Christian living, is to lead our internal parts from this core.

One person might be created with a musical part while another person might have a humorous part and yet another might have a studious part. We all have lots of these unburdened parts. When our internal experience is perfectly functioning, these parts are unhindered and fluid. By fluid, I mean they move into our immediate awareness when needed and move back out again when not.

Of course, we don't live in a perfect world. Hurts happen, injustices prevail, and the memory of pain lingers in mind and body. That pain hurts our parts and creates what we will call exiles.

EXILES

Exiles are the sensitive, hurting parts who carry the memory and the marks of pain from our past. We might have experienced humiliation, disappointment, grief, terror, or abandonment, either from an event or from a person. And let's be honest—we *all* have experienced pain in one way or another, so we all have exiles. Plenty of them.

Exile: A part that has become burdened by negative life experiences and has therefore lost access to its naturally positive qualities. Exiles carry negative emotions like fear, shame, loneliness, anxiety, and sadness, as well as negative beliefs such as "I'm all alone," "My feelings and needs don't matter," and "Something is wrong with me."

But who wants to keep feeling all those bad things? No one! We try to keep these vulnerable parts hidden away, pushed down, locked up, and sometimes entirely (we think) left behind.

Now you see why the term *exile* is so apt.

IFS uses the term *burdened* to describe the exile's encumbered state. Burdens are extreme ideas or feelings that are carried by parts and govern their lives. It's as if the part is now shackled with an emotional load (like sorrow, rejection, or loneliness) or a cognitive load (e.g., negative beliefs like "I'm not good enough," "I'm not worthy of a positive relationship," or "My feelings and need don't matter").

Burdens: Extreme feelings, beliefs, or behaviors that attach to parts as a result of negative life experiences. A burden is like a shackled weight that attaches to a part (thus, transforming it into an exile or a protector), causing the part to lose access to its naturally created positive essence.

Our parts weren't designed to carry these loads, which prevent them from being what they were designed to be. For example, a burdened part of us might lose access to its natural playfulness under a load of shame and fear. Because these parts carry our pain, we often try to make them go away so we can't feel how much they hurt.

The vulnerabilities of exiles in turn burden other parts, who then have to worry about keeping the exile's pain away from rest of the internal "family." As you would predict, now these burdened parts are also prevented from being what they were designed to be.

In IFS, we call these hard-working parts protectors because they are trying so hard to protect us from our exiles' pain.

PROTECTORS

Protector parts have two different strategies to try to prevent us from feeling our exiles' pain. One is proactive: parts that use these strategies are called managers. The other is reactive: parts that use these strategies are called firefighters.

Managers work in a variety of proactive ways to fend off pain, sometimes through performing at a high level, people pleasing, or putting everyone else's needs first. Firefighters rush in reactively to try to put out pain that is already there. Commonly, they rely on alcohol, drugs, dissociation, cutting, suicidality, rage, sexual acting out, or a variety of other impulsive options to make the pain go away.

Protectors show up in our lives in pretty predictable ways: The part that says under your breath while you raid the hotel minibar again, *I so deserve this.* The part of you that starts cleaning your office instead of tackling that looming deadline. The compulsion to be the life of the party when that's not who you are at all. The rage in you that puts a fist through a wall.

Yep. Protectors all, just trying to do their job: eradicate your pain.

The "solutions" that protector parts bring do lessen the pain for a time. Ultimately, though, they make our pain worse. And the amazing "Aha!" moment comes when we realize that even if they are doing destructive things, protector parts are sincerely trying to help and don't necessarily have awareness of other options or ways of behaving. They often don't like what they are doing but feel like it's all up to them to keep the pain at bay.

There is a crazy paradox here. Well-intentioned protectors try to shield us from pain and wind up contributing to it. A manager can succeed so well that we experience social isolation because no one can get past our Nice Guy cover-up to the real person underneath. A firefighter can bring quick relief but put us at real risk—of addiction, broken relationships, even death.

Protectors: Parts in a system that have become burdened with extreme roles in an attempt to eliminate exile pain. There are two types of protectors: managers, that try to proactively prevent exile pain from becoming activated, and firefighters, that try to reactively extinguish exile pain once it has been triggered.

Activated: When a part feels threatened (either by experiencing something that reminds it of a past hurt, or by the activity of a polarized part) and begins to flood, or take over, an individual's internal system.

In all this strange naming of the many aspects of our inner worlds that we may not have even known we had, let's remember our goal. What we're after are new, proven insights about our inner lives that don't contradict age-old, revealed truths. Insights that set us free in ways we had begun to think would *never* happen. That help us solve the puzzle of those hated feelings and behaviors that keep hurting us and those we love.

The terms may be unfamiliar, but since our old ways aren't working, it makes sense that a new way would require some new types of understanding.

In fact, I hope that this reimagining of who you are inside, and how the many aspects of your nature relate to each other, is spurring curiosity to dig further. If you're like me, you may have spent years beating yourself up for the behavior of one troublesome part or another. Or believing that the despicable behavior a part of you was engaged in is who you actually *are.*

Imagine with me how your life could be different if you really believed that the behavior you struggle the most with, or the feeling of which you are most ashamed, is not actually who you are. "What if," as Schwartz writes, "you totally trusted that those parts were different from your true Self and that you, as that Self, could help them to transform?"[8]

OREO BATTLES

To really wrap our heads around how our burdened parts function, let's go back to the idea of dieting and look at how opposing protector parts rush in to try to help. American media and pop culture are phenomenal at convincing us that we are fat and making us feel so bad about ourselves that we binge on Oreos. So let's go with that. I'll bet we've all been there.

Have you tried to go on a diet and found yourself embroiled in a nasty inner war? One part of you wants to lose weight, while another part wants to eat cookies? *In their own way, both parts are just trying to help you avoid feeling pain.*

A manager part that wants to lose weight might be ultraorganized, disciplined, and goal oriented. Think of it as the Clipboard Carrying Monitor—and trust me, it intends to tally every calorie you put in your mouth and plan every workout from now till next summer. Or perhaps the manager part is nasty, self-critical, and mean. In that case, call it the Internal Critic. It slouches around in there, letting fly with mean attacks about how ugly and disgusting you are. Both of these managers are trying in their own ways to prevent you from feeling the shame of gaining weight.

On the other hand, a firefighter part that wants to eat cookies may be impulsive and pleasure seeking with no concern for consequences. It has the temperament of an impulsive teenager. It wants what it wants when it wants it. And what it wants most is to help you stop feeling shame or pain by way of the pleasure of a sugar rush.

Notice how normal it is for these different protector parts to have unique and distinct identities. And oh my word, do they hate each other!

If you are like most people, your protector part with the clipboard is super strong and in charge for the first couple of weeks. (Or maybe days. Or hours. No judgment here, just keeping it real.) For however long this protector is in charge, you put every last calorie into your MyFitnessPal tracker and monitor your activity levels. You diligently check what your graphs and charts look like and, that evening, see if you have enough of a gap to eat three unsalted almonds for dessert.

The job of this protector part is to also keep the cookie-eating part of you locked in the basement. But before long, that cookie-eating part feels more and more deprived, and more and more angry. Finally, it gets so hacked that it bursts out of the basement in a fury and announces, "I'm taking over here, punk! You can toss that clipboard or I'll break it in half!" Then the cookie-eating part proceeds to take over, pushing the dieting part out of the way and eating the entire bag of Oreos. In ten minutes.

It ain't pretty, folks.

Now all that remains are the crumbs, one fat cookie eater, and a cowering protector with a broken clipboard. But we're not finished.

Right about now the third protector part shows up: the manager we've called the Internal Critic. And it starts yelling and heaping shame on the part that just ate the cookies. "You fat slob! What's the matter with you, eating that whole box of cookies? You are so worthless."

> Our burdened parts are struggling to avoid pain. Yet at our center is a calm, creative, and confident God Image, ready to help us transform.

On and on it goes. Most of us go through life clueless about this internal wrangling. We're pulled in one direction, then pushed in another, never figuring out who we really are or what we really want. And least of all, how to make our best self an enduring reality.

The insights of IFS change all that.

Once we see the larger picture, real change becomes possible. We begin to understand that our burdened parts, struggling to protect us from pain, are trapped in conflict. Yet we also see that at our center is a calm, creative, and confident God Image, ready to help us transform.

We have been to Oz and seen behind the curtain.

Now we know what's really going on. And we can begin to find our way home.

GOD OF PARTS?

With all the new terminology we are tossing around, you might be wondering: *Does this approach line up with scripture, or is this some woo-woo weirdness?*

I believe it does line up with scripture, and we will continue to unpack that in the pages ahead. But for now, consider this: The God of scripture manifests himself to the world in parts as well.

You know: God the Father, God the Son, and God the Holy Spirit. Just thinking about the Trinity gives most of us a brain cramp. But what if there's a kind of mirroring between God's essential nature and ours? Come to think of it, why *wouldn't* there be?

One of the best-known scenes from the creation story captures a conversation between God and, well, God. Remember in Genesis 1:26, we're told, "Then God said, 'Let *us* make mankind in *our* image, in *our* likeness" (emphasis mine). When theologians make the case for a three-in-one God, they start here. I still remember the illustration I heard in a children's sermon years ago. God is sort of like an egg: one egg, three parts—shell, yoke, and white. One God, three parts—Father, Son, and Holy Spirit.

The next verse shows why it makes sense that we would reflect the multifaceted nature of God. "So God created mankind in his own image, in the image of God he created them; male and female he created them." We are all created in the image of God. Not just any God—a God of parts.

There's a further parallel in Paul's explanation of how God expects the church to function. Paul wrote:

> Just as a body, though one, has many parts, but all its many parts form one body, so it is with Christ. . . .
>
> God has placed the parts in the body, every one of them, just as he wanted them to be. If they were all one part, where would the body be? *As it is, there are many parts, but one body.*
>
> The eye cannot say to the hand, "I don't need you!" And the head cannot say to the feet, "I don't need you!" . . . If one part suffers, every part suffers with it; if one part is honored, every part rejoices with it.
>
> Now you are the body of Christ, and each one of you is a part of it.[9]

Turns out this parts thing shows up a lot with God: One God with three parts. One church with many parts. One body with many parts. One person with many parts. In each case, the whole is greater than the sum of the parts.

Who we are inside will always remain a bit of a mystery. But mystery is not the same as disorder. Or brokenness. Or being bad to the bone. If we are created in the image of God, how could "bad" be who we are at our innermost?

That's one reason we can say with utter confidence that you have no bad parts, just good parts stuck in bad roles.

STANDING ON THE THRESHOLD

We are standing on the threshold of the clarity and hope we've been longing for. We know now that we are not one monolithic person. So when we have a part that is frequently provoked, we don't have to identify as "an angry person." When a part struggles to say no, we aren't "a people pleaser." When a part yells at the kids, we don't have to believe "I'm such a bad mom." Our parts are not who we are. We just have good parts stuck in bad roles.

There are no bad parts, only good parts stuck in bad roles.

If you just freaked out, taking this statement as some kind of disguised justification for doing anything you want and throwing truth out the window, well, at least you're paying attention. But that's not what I'm saying at all.

Not all *behaviors* are good, but all *parts* are. There's a huge difference. And as you'll see, acting on this important insight can help us stop bad behaviors and hold self-compassion in a much more effective way.

Discussion Questions

- How does the idea that your parts are not all of who you are help you access deeper self-compassion?

- We are just beginning to explore the concept, but what is it like for you to consider that there are no bad parts, only good parts stuck in bad roles?

- What is one protector within you that you can see as trying to protect you from pain? Where did it learn to try to help you with pain in this way?

- Have you ever experienced a time in your life when God has turned your image of him on its head and revealed a new, greater picture of himself to you?

WHERE IS GOD IN ALL MY MESS?

Surrendering to God's image
at our core

T his idea of being truly, deeply beautiful in our innermost self is new to many of us. And oh, so appealing. But it may also feel wrong, particularly for those of us who have been raised to believe that what we really are deep down is bad. Permanently broken. To us, a gentler perspective may feel suspiciously convenient and probably heretical.

In the previous chapter I described the inner, unchanging core of a person as the true self (in IFS language) or God Image (from our faith perspective). In this chapter, we'll explore what being made in the image of God means for our healing journey, what it means to have the divine signature on our innermost being. To experience the possibility of God In Here, rather than God Over There.

This discussion is critical, my friend. Where is God when we're floundering in self-destructive feelings and behaviors? What does it mean to be saved—and what if I keep on struggling like crazy thereafter? Can I really believe that there's an unalterable goodness at my core?

Any truly helpful understanding of our parts or hope for realizing the joy and peace at our core must begin here.

Let's acknowledge that these are huge, ridiculously loaded topics, and thoughtful people hold differing opinions. Are we bad to the bone—thank you, Adam and Eve? Are we shaped by evolution to be selfish creatures bent only on survival? Or is who we are inside created mainly by how we were raised or what we experienced in our formative years?[10]

This chapter proposes one possibility for you to consider—one that happens to parallel the IFS model. Whether you understand it primarily from a biblical perspective or primarily from intuition and experience, I hope that by the end of this chapter you'll see new vistas and new possibilities opening up for you.

Most of all, I hope you receive for yourself the incredible compassion Jesus showed toward our fundamental essence.

HOW FAR AWAY IS GOD WHEN . . . ?

It may be those of us on a lifelong journey as Christians who most need permission to see God and ourselves with fresh eyes. I'm not sure why that is. Maybe we become so closely identified with a familiar set of beliefs that new, larger understandings just can't get in.

In my experience, what I call the God Over There view is deeply ingrained in faith culture, even when we give lip service to other beliefs. *God Over There* implies that I must do something—probably a lot—before I can get over my pile of sin and truly rest in his presence and enjoy his favor.

If my idea of God is that my huge pile of sin is standing in the way of that happening, I just might give up and go have a latte.[11] Because my pile is huge. And I don't have a shovel that big.

Just between you and me, I think this is how many of us see God. God Over There. Or Up There somewhere. Definitely nowhere near that awful pile of my sin. Sure, he loves me—it seems like he kinda has to. But when this is my view of God, I always have a sneaking suspicion that he doesn't really *like* me very much.

And actually, it's even worse than that.

I mean, can you imagine how far away from me God must be when I'm stuck? When "what I want to do I do not do, but what I hate I do"?[12]

Let's say I'm battling anxiety. (In IFS terms we'd say that a scared exile part of me is burdened with anxiety/fear and keeps getting activated.) And let's say I hear—correctly—that perfect love casts out all fear.[13] Jesus is perfect love.[14] That would mean if I'm in complete communion with Jesus, I won't feel that nasty, yucky anxiety.

But hold on. Something doesn't add up. After all, God put the capacity for those negative feelings within me in the first place. Not only that, when he created them he said they were "very good."[15] Those yucky, scary feelings are good.

Sit with this for a minute: your fear is *good*.

Difficult feelings—in this case, fear—are *qualitatively* good. Notice I didn't say they *feel* good. But they are important messengers, and God didn't place the capacity for negative feelings in my brain so he could shame me for feeling them.

Or distance himself from me until I stopped feeling those feelings.

Or until I stopped doing really dumb, sinful things that are probably rooted in those feelings.

Fear (or any other negative emotion) comes out of my experience, and it's there for good reason. I didn't just wake up and decide to be fearful one day. Either I'm actually in danger, or there is something unhealed in my life that created the fear, and that experience lives on in the limbic (feeling) part of my brain which is not in communication with the cortex (thinking) part of my brain. *No communicado.*

> God didn't place the capacity for negative feelings in my brain so he could shame me for feeling them.

At least not when I'm actually feeling the fear.

So, what I know to be true is largely irrelevant when I'm in the experience of fear, other than to add to my shame because I am feeling something I think I shouldn't feel. Now I feel afraid *and* like a bad person for feeling it. Most of us don't know enough about neurochemistry to realize that to expect otherwise is lunacy.

What would it mean for us if God is already In Here? In you? In me? Literally, *in the mess with us*? What if, when we're struggling with anxiety and fear and other bad feelings, we didn't have to get Over There to him?

What if he were already right here in you and in me and not a millimeter farther away *while we're experiencing those bad feelings*?

GOD IN THE MESS WITH US

I believe Genesis 1:27 speaks right to this point: "So God created mankind in his own image, in the image of God he created them; male and female he created them."

Think about it: God's image, his very likeness within every human being as a birthright. Why wouldn't God's likeness in our being be the seat of all true wisdom and peace and healing? Kind of like a power receptor waiting to be plugged in when we receive the power and filling of the Holy Spirit.

And this is where faith and clinical IFS experience converge. It turns out that this God Image within each person remains fundamentally undamaged, regardless of the amount of abuse or neglect or trauma that the individual may have suffered, and no matter what kinds of unhelpful coping strategies they have developed.

In other words, parts of our human selves—what we're calling exiles and protectors—carry the sin and pain we experience in life, but deep within every one of us resides the fingerprint of God. By virtue of the fact that it reveals the likeness of God, that fingerprint cannot be tainted or broken. The parts of us that are holding sin are not part of our God Image. They can't be. Our God Image is the very image of God, who is by definition unbroken.

But wait. Aren't we sinners at our core and fundamentally depraved?

What I'm saying is, yes. And no. Our God Image is not distorted, but our burdened parts are.

God created humans in his own image, and once he completed man and woman, he said it was not just good, but very good. Adam and Eve lived in perfect communion with God, with no sin. No depravity. Which means no burdened parts.

Free will, yes.

Depravity, no.

Whether we choose to interpret the creation account literally or metaphorically, it appears that prior to the Fall and the arrival of sin, Adam and Eve had a God Image at their core and unburdened parts of them that constituted their unique personalities, but no burdened parts that would separate them from the God Image within and without.

Then sin entered the picture and immediately some parts became burdened; they became what we will call exiles like shame and fear, or protectors like hiding and blaming. Sin is the burden that some of our God-Image core. We'll get to know exiles and protectors better in the following chapters, but they were not who Adam and Eve fundamentally were because sin was not powerful enough to destroy the image of God within them. Or within us. But exiles and protectors showed up when sin and brokenness entered the picture. They are our parts that carry the effects of sin and the fallen world,

Sin is the burden that some of our parts carry, but it does not tarnish our God-Image core.

and they hijack our inner system. When they hijack our lives, we are separated from both the God Image within and the experience of God outside of us.

Look at the familiar Genesis 3 account with your new parts understanding in mind, and I think you'll see what I mean.

"Then the eyes of both of them were opened, and they realized they were naked."[16]

Translation: "Oh, no!"

Exile #1: Shame.

" . . . So they sewed fig leaves together and made coverings for themselves."[17]

Protector #1: Hiding.

"Then the man and his wife heard the sound of the LORD God as he was walking in the garden in the cool of the day, and they hid from the LORD God among the trees of the garden."[18]

Protector #1: Hiding 2.0.

"But the LORD God called to the man, 'Where are you?'"

"He answered, 'I heard you in the garden, and I was afraid because I was naked; so I hid.'"[19]

Exile #2: Fear.

"And he said, 'Who told you that you were naked? Have you eaten from the tree that I commanded you not to eat from?'"[20]

Have you seen the dog videos when the owner comes home and the whole house is torn apart? And the dog has down feathers coming out of its mouth, and the owner says "Fido, did you eat the couch?" And Fido tries to appear really innocent and looks over as if to blame it on the cat?

Yeah. That's Adam in this moment. He tells God, "The woman you put here with me—she gave me some fruit from the tree, and I ate it."[21]

Protectors #2 and #3: Blaming and Play the Victim.

(You know it's rough when you start your first day of sin blaming God for what you did wrong.)

"Then the LORD God said to the woman, 'What is this you have done?'"

"The woman said, 'The serpent deceived me, and I ate.'"[22]

Protector #2: Blame 2.0.

And now Adam and Eve had parts that were burdened with sin. Thus began the legacy of sin/burdened parts separating humanity from the God Image that resides right within us and that enables free-flowing communion with the divine. While we can bring healing to some of our burdened parts, as long as we are on this side of heaven we will never be completely free from parts with burdens.

Yet the image of God that was in Adam and Eve's souls from the beginning has never been altered because it is the very reflection of God, and God by his fundamental nature remains pure, holy, untarnished, without burden, whole.

SALVATION: THE LIVED EXPERIENCE OF GOD'S LOVE

But if those who don't yet know the power of Jesus in their lives still have an essential, deep essence in them that longs for glory, what about a saving relationship with Jesus? What does that change? Where does that come into play?

I would explain salvation like this: There's a God Image in me as a condition of my birth. (That's probably the very thing that causes my heart to be drawn to a relationship with him—because I'm made for him.) When I invite Christ into my heart and life through an act of faith, God's likeness in me prepares and empowers me to receive a new spiritual birth in Christ.

I am now living an *experience of* God's love, not just a *knowing about* it. He is filling me up inside with his divine essence.

Paul beautifully describes this fullness of God in people who know Jesus as "Christ *in you*, the hope of glory" (emphasis mine).[23] First John 4:4 states it like this: "The one who is *in you* is greater than the one who is in the world" (emphasis mine).

When I program "God" into my Waze app, it says, "You have arrived." I'm already to God because he's In Here. This matters because now the hurting, stuck parts of me—my exiles and protectors—have a place to go to find healing, to be unburdened, and to be transformed without having to change their ZIP code to locate it. They don't have to try or work or do anything except *be* in the presence of God within. Yes, of course he is omnipresent, but for the purposes of how I can personally relate to him, he is already In Here, in my core self.

> When I program "God" into my Waze app, it says, "You have arrived."

You may have parts that are thinking, *"This sounds like a spiritual sales pitch. You're telling me to do* the reverse *of what I've always been taught to do to connect with God? I'm supposed to just relax into it?"*

I get it. But I'm simply conveying what scripture has been telling us all along.

When God promises in both the Old and New Testaments, "I will never leave you; I will never forsake you,"[24] he's saying, "I will never leave you because I am In Here, not Out There—where I might be tempted to run out and grab a sandwich. No! I go where you go. Because I am with you, in you, your only hope of glory."[25]

Perhaps this is why Paul seemed so utterly, emphatically convinced that "neither death nor life, neither angels nor demons, neither the present nor the future, nor any powers, neither height nor depth, nor anything else in all creation, will be able to separate us from the love of God that is in Christ Jesus our Lord."[26]

This is pretty significant because if our inner being is inseparable from God's love, our whole strategy for closeness to God changes. It's no longer about striving to get to God Over There, and all about surrendering to God In Here.

In fact, all that striving actually takes us *further* from an authentic experience of God, because it's a striving protector part that has become a roadblock to the God Image. To what is within us all along. (More on this in chapters 6 and 9, where we explore our Spiritualizer part.)

THE EIGHT CS AND THE FRUIT OF THE SPIRIT

Let me tell you the amazing way Schwartz identified what he called the undamaged Self when the Imago Dei was the furthest thing from his mind.

He asked.

He talked to clients, discovered their parts, then gently invited the parts that he was meeting to "step back" or "unblend" from the person. And *voilà*! After all the parts had finally stepped back, a healthy, positive Self emerged. Clear as day, even though he was totally surprised to discover it. And it felt the same in every client, to the degree that he began identifying the characteristics that were present when clients were in Self. Sure enough, the qualities of this Self were consistently what we'd describe as good—qualities like curiosity, compassion, courage, connection, clarity, calm, confidence, and creativity.

Unblend: The process whereby a blended part feels safe enough, or relaxed enough, to release control and step back from the central experience of the individual. When a part unblends, the person will notice an abating of its emotions, sensations, and thoughts from their immediate awareness. (Synonyms: *step back, separate, relax.*)

After Schwartz encountered what he would come to call the Eight Cs within each of his clients (and, of course, himself) when all their parts had stepped back, he began to realize this is an unchanging truth: a core Self, in his words, that is within everyone. When people were in full communion with their Self, they didn't have to manufacture or create the good qualities; those qualities just spontaneously emerged.

Schwartz concluded that these qualities are always present in every individual, but that people lose access to them if wounded or protective parts of the individual get in the way by stepping up and taking control of the person. If the Self was metaphorically sitting in a chair, it's as though the parts step in front of it so that the essence of the Self can no longer shine through. The Self is still there, just obscured.

As I understand this phenomenon through the lens of faith, the Self within that Schwartz refers to is our connectivity to God. It's our *authentic* spirituality.

As long as we are on the topic of authentic spirituality, you've noticed I'm sure that the Schwartz's Eight Cs sound an awful lot like the fruit of the Spirit: love, joy, peace, patience, kindness, goodness, faithfulness, gentleness, and self-control.[27]

This spiritual fruit is accessed, Galatians 5:16 tells us, when we "walk by the Spirit." In other words, when our parts have stepped back and we "walk by the God Image" (not walking Over There to get to the Spirit*)*, these qualities will spontaneously emerge, just as Schwartz discovered with his clients.

John 15:4–5 is so much clearer to me now. In preparation for his departure, Jesus tells his followers:

"Remain in me, as I also remain in you. No branch can bear fruit by itself; it must remain in the vine. Neither can you bear fruit unless you remain in me.

"I am the vine; you are the branches. If you remain in me and I in you, you will bear much fruit."

I've heard so many sermons on these two verses, insisting that the fruit of the Spirit is not something I can manufacture, but is something that spontaneously emerges when I am "in the vine."

The concept of surrender and release into the fruit never made sense to me when I understood that God was on the other side of my sins or my best efforts or, for that matter, on the other side of my most deeply felt worship experience. But I've learned that if my parts have all stepped back and I have full access to the fruit of the Spirit that is already within me, well then, that's a different matter altogether. The fruit spontaneously overflows. And I can exhale. I can surrender into the God Image at the core of my being.

Schwartz calls this accessing the Self. I like to call it prayer. Or worship.

You know when you have access to your God Image. You feel it. It's physical. It's the seamless communion with God that we were designed to live with in Eden. Sin and brokenness happened, so our parts became burdened. Now they take over and keep me away from that wordless communion a lot of the time.

But not because God left me. Not for one minute. He's right in my core. And yours.

Immanuel.

Going Deeper: Accessing your God Image*

I invite you to try a brief exercise to see if you can access your God Image. We can do it together, right here, right now. But I've gotta say, with great honor and gratitude for any work your industrious parts might be doing, please respect your parts. If at any point anything experiential feels uncomfortable because your parts are getting activated, stop and do whatever healthy thing you need to do to take care of yourself.

Get comfortable, close your eyes, and turn your attention inward. Focus on what you are feeling and experiencing.

Think of a person who mildly irritates you. Please don't choose your worst enemy or anyone who has really hurt you. Be gentle. Keep it manageable. Maybe choose someone who has lied to you, or a person who gets on your nerves.

Now, imagine that person is in a room, and you are outside the room looking in at them through a one-way window. Pause and use all of your senses to really notice this person in the room. Now gently check in with yourself. How do you feel *toward* them? Angry? Detached? Afraid? Judgmental?

---

* Exercise adapted from *Introduction to the Internal Family Systems Model,* by Dr. Richard Schwartz.

Once you know what you are feeling, *shift your focus to that feeling* and ask if it would be willing to separate from you a little bit. Just for a minute. Remember, you are still outside the room. (Okay, I know it's weird to talk to a feeling that way but humor me.)

If, after you ask the feeling to separate (or step back) from you, you sense a withdrawal of the energy of that feeling, notice what emotion or thought comes up next about that person in the room.

If the next thing that comes up for you is not curiosity, acceptance, and compassion (in other words, not coming from your God Image), then ask that next feeling or thought to separate as well. If you don't sense a fading of these emotions or thoughts, ask them what they are afraid would happen if they did step back. Those parts probably have a good reason not to want to move aside and leave you vulnerable to that person again.

Keep in mind that sleepiness, distraction or wandering thoughts, worry that you are not doing it right, and skepticism about this exercise are all parts. Treat them like you would any other part. Welcome that skepticism, for example. Let it know you appreciate how it's trying to help you. Ask what it is afraid would happen if you weren't skeptical. You get the idea.

You might need to remind these parts that you're not going in the room or taking any risks with this person in real life. You just want to get an idea of what happens when they let you, in your God Image, be present outside the room.

If your parts did step back, you might have begun to spontaneously experience qualities of your God Image emerging. You might have suddenly felt curious about why the person acted the way he or she did. Or you were able to see the situation from that person's perspective and better understand their behavior. Maybe you still didn't want to get near them but felt less of a need to change him or her. The person's image might have changed, maybe becoming less irritating or scary.[28]

Different, isn't it? But if your parts were willing to step back and give you access to your God Image, you felt how beautiful it is.

If we took it a step further, once you had access to your God Image—by inviting all the parts that are present to step back, or unblend—your God Image could actually have a healing experience with these parts.

Perhaps you had a part that was afraid of the person in the room. With great tenderness, your God Image could ask that fearful part how it came to be afraid and what it needed to feel safe. That part could share its experience without fear of judgment or pressure to change, and then experience the love, safety, and compassion of the power of God within you and be calmed and healed.

Most of us have no experience relating to ourselves or our parts or God this way. If you were given access to your God Image, notice and write down how effective this experience was in calming your negative emotions toward that person.

FLOWING OUT OF YOUR BEING

Scripture extends the same invitation. John 7:38–39 says it sweetly: "'Whoever believes in me, as Scripture has said, rivers of living water will flow from within them.' By this he meant the Spirit."

So, we have these streams of living water within us. Within our God Image. Therefore, we also have at all times the ability to do what I call a Spiritual MRI—a one-question self-check that asks, "How do I feel *toward* this part, person, or experience?"

Spiritual MRI: Noticing how one feels *toward* a part, person, or experience. Any feelings that do not reflect the Eight Cs indicate there is a part blended and the individual does not have access to their core God Image.

If our answer is calm, curious, compassionate, and/or connected, we are probably responding from our spiritual core. If our answer is anything else (defensive, skeptical, scared, angry, frustrated), we know we have a part or parts in charge.

When we approach these parts with gentle compassion and respect for the hard work they are doing, they could be willing to unblend from us enough to share their story and give us access to our God Image. The way is now paved for our exiles to run to our God Image for comfort and healing.

Now I have a whole different way of understanding Matthew 11:28: "Come to me, all you who are weary and burdened, and I will give you rest."

The process is gentle by which we respectfully and lovingly bring awareness to our parts and allow them such honor that they become willing to unblend and give us access to the God within us.

Now *this* is grace.

Discussion Questions

- What thoughts come to mind when you reflect on the statement, "God didn't place the capacity for negative feelings in my brain so he could shame me for feeling them"?

- How can grasping that God is In Here instead of Over There change the way you relate with him?

- Even though we have been given the power of the Spirit, why do we feel the need to get closer to Jesus by our own power, in your opinion? How has living that way worked for you?

- In the "Going Deeper: Accessing your God Image" exercise, what did you experience? Were your parts willing to unblend? If not, what were they concerned might happen if they did? If you gained access to your God Image, what emotions or thoughts were you aware of?

LISTENING WELL
TO OUR EXILES

Hope for our hurting parts

All this talk about God Image sounds good, but I don't go through life just bubbling over with confidence, compassion, clarity, and courage. If I'm really honest, what defines my life more often is pain, loneliness, even numbness—sometimes in ways that really worry me.

It's true. We usually don't walk around just overflowing with the fruit of the Spirit, even though our God Image is always present at our core. Sometimes we overflow with painful thoughts, feelings, and emotions. Why is that? Well, maybe a lesson in leprosy can help us understand.

Leprosy? We in contemporary America don't know much about this horrible disease, but since ancient times those who suffered from it were excluded from normal society. In biblical times, and in a culture where ritual cleanliness was the measure of spiritual state, sufferers had to live in isolation or call out "unclean" everywhere they went. Having a family or normal life of any kind was out of the question.

Jesus had great compassion for people with leprosy.[29] He understood that their suffering was rooted in a strange condition.

They didn't feel pain.

Now, normally we are all in favor of not feeling pain. We take pills. We drink and drug and act out sexually to escape it. We lose ourselves in TV and volunteering and staying busy. We do not like pain.

It turns out that leprosy deadens pain. The disease does that by killing nerve endings, and as a result people get hurt. They lose parts of their body and suffer disfigurement and ugly discoloration from burns and other injuries. Because if you can't feel pain, you don't know when something is wrong.

> If you can't feel pain, you don't know when something is wrong.

You don't want to miss this.

For most of the world, leprosy is not a thing anymore, at least for our bodies. But in our hearts, I'd say we suffer from a virtual epidemic. We do not want to feel pain. Or discomfort. Or any type of negative emotion at all.

Somewhere along the line, we've missed the reality that our negative emotions are among the most important guides to our inner health—if we listen to them.

In chapter 2 we identified the original, true you, a part we described as your God Image. When we surrender into this enduring, spiritual core, we regain access to innate gifts like courage, confidence, and clarity, among others. In this chapter and the next, we look at parts that often stand in the way of living out of that strength, in particular the parts that have been shaped by pain and our continuing response to it. We call them exiles, which as you learned in chapter 2 are burdened parts of us that carry old pain.

Once we understand these hurting parts and how they sometimes dominate our lives, we can stop being so afraid of them and instead learn to have compassion for their pain. In fact, we can begin to free them from their suffering altogether.

I'll show you how.

LISTENING WELL TO THE GIFT OF PAIN

I work a lot with brave clients who are struggling with addiction. Even if you don't deal with addiction all day, you probably know as well as I do that addiction is a cunning and baffling foe. Addiction is the one disease that tells you that you don't have a disease. It lies and tells you everything is fine and "You've got this" and you can go right on ahead and have that drink because "You can control it this time."

Yeah. You so don't have this. You can't control it.

Do you know what is usually required to stop the inevitable, downward, devastating spiral of addiction?

Pain. Yes. The gift of pain. You read that right. I just called pain a G-I-F-T.

In my work, when an addict experiences pain at a level that makes them feel they can't go on, we say they are "hitting bottom."

Hitting bottom and seeing someone we love hit bottom are a very difficult things. Why? Because none of us like pain. People started drinking or drugging or watching porn in the first place because those seem like ways to avoid pain. Probably that's why people who love that person try to help in various ways. Unfortunately, when loving family and friends try to rescue their loved ones from the consequences of their addiction, they remove the gift of pain.

What happens then? The addiction persists and grows stronger, and the bottom gets lower. Every time.

I know this might sound heartless, but taking away pain is actually the cruelest thing we can do for someone caught in the grip of addiction. Every courageous person in long-term recovery will tell you how grateful she is for her own personal "bottom." For the "I can't take this anymore" moment when she surrendered, cried out to God, and reached out for help. Looking back, she knows the pain of hitting bottom likely saved her life.

We don't know why something's wrong, and we can't wisely seek help until we feel and experience and listen well to the gift of our pain. And that's not only true with addiction.

I need to listen to my anger to know that I've had a boundary violated.

I need to listen to my loneliness to know that I need to invest in deep relationships.

I need to listen to my anxiety to know that I have an unresolved trauma that needs to heal.

I need to listen to my depression to know that I need care for my heart's deepest wounds.

I need to listen to my fear to know that I may need to create safety.

I need to listen to my stress and irritability to know that I'm out of balance and need rest or reprioritization.

One common experience, however, keeps us all stuck. Instead of moving *toward* our pain and listening to the valuable messages it has for us, the vast majority of us move *against* or *away* from it. We ignore it, deny it, feel ashamed for feeling it, resent it, or attempt to numb, deflect, or dismiss it.

We've been well taught to not listen to, or even feel, those yucky, hard feelings.

Suck it up, buttercup.

Be a man.

Big girls don't cry.

Stop your whining or I'll give you something to whine about!

You can see why I believe we suffer from a very serious leprosy of the heart. And it's killing us.

But what if instead of moving against or away from the pain we feel, we moved *toward* it? That's what Jesus invited us to do and modeled with his life. He stepped into the world and moved toward the people in the most pain, with the most sorrow, with the biggest hurts. He moved toward them and heard their stories, let them know they were not alone, and brought healing to them through touch and comfort and witnessing.

What if we did within our hearts what Jesus did outside them—*moved toward the pain and hurt and actually listened to it?*

AN EXILE'S GOTTA HURT

Exiles are the tender, hurting, vulnerable parts of us that feel all our difficult emotions. Think shame, worthlessness, terror, grief, loss, depression, loneliness, neediness, anxiety, pain, powerlessness, fear, and isolation. We come by them honestly, even though they weren't part of God's perfect original design.

God designed us for a perfect world—a world of unhindered, intimate, vulnerable communion with God and with others. No pain. No tears. No sin. No brokenness. And scripture tells us that heaven awaits us with unburdened bliss.

But in the meantime, we live in a world with pain and brokenness. Lots and lots of brokenness. So, we have exiles. In IFS, we call them exiles because these tender parts have been wounded the most. But the name captures another important reality: our protector parts work really hard to *keep them exiled*. Keep them hiding in the dark recesses of our souls. Ignore them. Starve them. Deprive them of companionship and compassion. Which is not the nicest way to care for someone in pain.

Exile: A part that has become burdened by negative life experiences and has therefore lost access to its naturally positive qualities. Exiles carry negative emotions like fear, shame, loneliness, anxiety, and sadness, as well as negative beliefs such as "I'm all alone," "My feelings and needs don't matter," and "Something is wrong with me."

Where do these exile parts come from originally? Why don't they get better or go away, despite our best efforts to get rid of them? Let's take a look.

Some exiles come from obvious places.

If in our lives, we witness violence (hitting, throwing, slamming doors, threatening, gunshots) in our home or community; if we are the targets of violence or bullying by a parent, sibling, or friend of the family; if we are called names or screamed at or told things were our fault when they weren't; or if we were touched in sexual ways or shown sexual images when we were young, or our developing bodies were the subject of inappropriate sexual jokes or observations, then we are likely to develop exiles that are frozen at the age of that experience and often feel powerlessness, terror, shame, and isolation.

If our parents were too engrossed in their own worlds to care for our emotional or physical needs, if they needed us to "make them okay" or emotionally caretake them, if we were too emotionally connected (enmeshed) with one parent because the other wasn't there or the marital relationship was conflicted, or if we were left alone to figure out life on our own, then we will likely develop exiles that feel alone, broken, overdependent, overresponsible, and angry.

I've just described for you the exile children of abuse, abandonment, neglect, and enmeshment. These types of adverse experiences are overt. They're obvious. Most of us can readily identify them.

Some exiles come to us in more indirect ways, yet they're every bit as real. I refer to them as stealth, or covert, exiles. They're not so obvious.

If we were raised in a loving home, neighborhood, or faith community, but one in which standards of perfection were modeled, where we weren't allowed to struggle with any "real" issues or "real" sin, where we had to be a size two, we had to be an A student, or we weren't allowed to do anything to embarrass Dad or Mom or the family name, then we will often develop exiles that feel not good enough. This is particularly real when Dad or Mom is a pastor, elder, deacon, or worship leader, and we grew up under the scrutiny and expectations of perfection from a congregation.

If we had a high performing or rebellious sibling who received all the parents' or culture's attention, we may develop exiles that feel unseen, less than, or unimportant.

If we had a sibling or family member who was chronically ill, we may develop exiles that believe, "My feelings and needs don't matter," because how can you have normal developmental angst when your sister or dad is in the hospital with cancer?

If we lived in homes or communities where violence was routine, lived through a natural disaster such as a flood or a tornado or a wildfire, or people we loved died, we may develop exiles that feel unsafe, helpless, or powerless.

If we were raised in homes where children were seen and not heard, we may develop exiles who believe, "I have no voice." Likewise, if we were raised in homes where children ran the show and the parents didn't parent, we may develop exiles that believe, "I am alone" and "It's up to me to figure everything out."

If we had parents who struggled with overspending and debt, and money was an ever-present and stressful topic, we may grow up with exiles that believe, "I'm not worth it," or "Money is more important than me."

If we had parents who were critical, had impossible standards, were shaming, made critical remarks about weight, criticized our performance, or never came to a game, we may develop exiles that feel bad, less than, not good enough, or broken.

If we were bullied in school, left out, or had a hard time making friends, we may develop exiles that feel unchosen, unseen, or broken.

Regardless of how the exiles developed, they matter and they are in pain. And when they are unhealed—or when we don't even know they are there—they will continue to *create new pain for us*, as well as *distort how we see the world* in a way that will negatively impact our behaviors.

Time does not heal exiles. We don't just spontaneously get over them. You may have heard said about a painful situation in a child's life—like divorce, a loved one's death, or abuse—"But kids are so resilient." And by *resilient*, the person means, "This difficult situation isn't really having that much of an impact on that child." Or, "He'll get over it."

May I tell you, emphatically, that is not true!

Children are not resilient in that sense of the word. They are often experiencing as much or more pain as the adults involved, but they have fewer coping strategies to survive. They may have figured out creative ways to numb their pain or keep it hidden, but visible and invisible exiles carry equal amounts of pain.

An exile is an exile. And please, do not assume the exiles of overt abuse and neglect are somehow more important or matter more than stealth exiles. In fact, sometimes the stealth exiles are particularly hard to recognize and embrace because we discount them.

"But I grew up in a loving family."

"But my parents were Christians and raised us in church."

"But all my physical needs were met."

"But I knew I was loved even if no one ever said it."

All of that may be true. But your pain still matters. Your exiles still hurt. If I get hit by a bus when I cross the street, I still have to go to the hospital even if the driver didn't mean to hit me and feels really bad about it. I'm still in the ICU. There's no shame in saying, "I was hit by a bus." But if I ignore the bus and my injuries and refuse to say that I was in an accident and don't go to the hospital, I'm likely not going to heal well, could develop a secondary infection, and will always walk with a limp. When we are hit by an emotional bus, the same principle holds true.

Getting to know our exiles is not about blaming anyone or casting a negative light on others. In all likelihood, the people who impacted our lives were well intentioned and doing the best they could with whatever exiles and protectors *they* had developed. Instead, getting to know our exiles is about making sense of our own stories. It's about speaking and honoring our truth.

Let me introduce you to some of my exiles, and as you get to know mine, maybe you'll meet some of your own.

WHEN A PERM ISN'T THE SOLUTION

I grew up in a loving home. I was told I was loved. All my physical needs were met. We went to church. I was not beaten or threatened. I had learning opportunities. We lived modestly but comfortably. I never wanted for any material need. But sure enough, a very real "bus" hit me, and my exiles have carried the pain all my life.[30]

I was an only child in a military family that moved every year or two. I had no siblings, no other kids (for a long time) on either side of my extended family, and no lasting friendships, because we never stayed in one place long. I was always on the outside looking in. Always the new kid who didn't belong.

I also took on the typical only-child role of hero in my family, so I had a lot of anxiety about doing everything perfectly. I was alone or surrounded by adults, I didn't fit in with other kids, and I was an awkward late bloomer.

What could possibly go wrong?

Just as I entered my tender teen years, we moved to Hawaii where haoles—Caucasian people like me—weren't particularly welcomed, and I found myself in an extremely high-performing private school where I could barely keep my head above water. Students at Punahou School had plenty of money, and they all seemed brilliant, beautiful, sophisticated, and extraordinarily talented. Not only had these students been together since kindergarten, but most of their parents had gone to that same private school together as well.

You might be familiar with some of the classmates at Punahou in grades near mine: Barack Obama, president of the United States; Steve Case, cofounder and former CEO of AOL; Albert Cheng, Emmy-winning COO of Amazon Studios; and Carrie Ann Inaba, judge on *Dancing with the Stars*.

You get the idea.

My middle-class, buck-toothed, dweeby military self didn't exactly fit in. I entered Punahou School immature and awkward, with acne, head-gear, and those little rubber bands that shoot out of your mouth and hit people if you yawn, smile, or open your mouth too wide.

And did I mention the perm? Back in the day, it was all the rage to have long, loopy curls cascading gently down the sides of your head so you could toss your hair casually while you laughed, and those magical curls would bounce gracefully off your shoulders. Since several of the girls in the school were (what else?) professional models, I thought per-haps a perm was the answer to my friend problem. If only I could have those wide, gently cascading locks, then I would be accepted.

I had discovered the answer! Except . . . we couldn't afford a salon perm.

Not to worry, my mom said. She'd endured many home perms, and although I was familiar with those stories and her catch phrase—"It's painful to be beautiful"—I eagerly agreed to a home perm compliments of Mom.

Now, my mom is talented at many, many things. But she is not, unfortunately, a professional beautician. And this was a key piece of information that my fourteen-year-old self failed to consider.

Mom and I went to the store and picked out a box perm and brought it home with enthusiastic anticipation of the wide, looping, friend-at-tracting curls that would be mine in just a few hours. Unpacking the contents of the box, however, I failed to take note of the teeny-weeny little curlers that were to set my new look. You see, I'd never been to a salon or had a perm.

So, when we decided to leave the solution on these teeny-weeny roll-ers "just a little extra" so that the perm would be sure to take, no alarm bells went off in my head.

If you already know what awaited me when I removed those teeny-weeny little over-set rollers from my hair, you are absolutely and completely correct: an Afro of majestic proportions. And there was no taming it.

If perm relaxers existed back in the eighties, I didn't know about them. The ringlets were so tight that I couldn't even pull them back into a ponytail, and clipping them back only succeeded in causing the ends to stick straight out from my head.

We did the only thing we could possibly do: got into the car, drove down to the local barber shop, and paid five dollars to get all of my hair cut off. Like, down-to-a-quarter-of-an-inch cut off. All the way around. Nothing left to style.

I cried for, gosh, I don't know, a year.

My almost-bald self made my way into this bastion of affluent brilliance every day thereafter with deep shame and self-loathing. There was no escape. It took until my senior year before I could at least mimic the ever-popular Farrah Fawcett flip style of that decade. And meantime, eating to numb my pain served only to make me bald and headgeared and, well, plump.

During those dark years, I was bullied and rejected, and I struggled academically and socially. As a result, I developed some pretty powerful exiles who carried negative core beliefs like "unchosen," "broken," "not good enough," "stupid," and "ugly." There were a few stretches in the worst of those years when my exiles were in so much pain, they thought not living looked pretty good compared to continuing to endure the torment.

Fast-forward a few decades and I did eventually grow into myself, went to Harvard, earned a couple of master's degrees, and developed many rich and enduring relationships.

Does any of that matter to these exiles?

Nope.

Not one bit.

They are frozen in time at age fourteen, and in spite of my best efforts at personal healing, I have to be honest and say they still hold some power over me. When I walk into a new environment, even though I'm fairly extroverted and confident, those exiles will sit up and start telling me how I'm not good enough or don't fit in. And I'm forty-nine years old. And a therapist.

Exiles are powerful.

MOVING TOWARD YOUR EXILES

We tend to cope with these hurting little ones by shaming them—"I can't believe I'm a grown woman feeling this way"—or shunning them, or trying our best to shut them up and lock them in the basement of our souls.

Let me ask you something: if your child came home and wanted to tell you about the rejection she faced at school that day, would you shame her? Tell her to go away? Ignore her efforts to get your attention?

Of course not! You'd pull up a chair, give her a hug, and tell her she is loved.

That's all our exiles want. They want to be seen and heard and cared for, and that's what Jesus does. He speaks to this in Matthew 11:28: "Come to me, all you who are weary and burdened, and I will give you rest."

Exiles want to be seen and heard and cared for, and that's what Jesus does.

Funny that the therapy term for the pain these exiles carry is *burden*. Suddenly, the healing power of this therapy model makes so much sense.

Unlike Jesus, we sometimes try to make the pain of exiles go away by:

- Locking them up. ("I don't know how I feel.")
- Staying too busy to have time for them. ("I've got so much on my plate. I can't slow down to feel.")
- Numbing them. ("I need a glass of wine. Or those cute shoes.")
- Locking them in the basement. ("I should quit whining; my problems don't matter. It's that guy with serious problems who has legitimate pain.")
- Spiritualizing them. ("A good Christian wouldn't feel this way.")

Not only are these responses heartless, they also don't work. They actually make the pain worse, because now the exiles feel shame for feeling shame.

We can't get rid of parts. And we don't want to! When they are healed, they spontaneously transform to bring something wonderful to our internal system. Often, when these wounded parts unburden ("find rest for their souls"), they bring joy, playfulness, tenderness, or spontaneity to our lives. They can also increase our capacity for genuine friendship, for experiencing and creating art, for soulfulness. In other words, in their own way, they are quite beautiful. But while they carry burdens, their positive qualities remain locked away, inaccessible. That explains why many of us who have wounded and still burdened exiles struggle to play, to be carefree, or to let people in to see who we really are.

Then Jesus, in true rebel fashion, shows up and says, "Let the little children come to me, and do not hinder them, for the kingdom of heaven belongs to such as these."[31]

For our conversation here, we might read Christ's invitation like this: *"Don't hinder the exiles! Don't lock them in the basement. Don't get in the way of their access to me. I want to scoop them up and hold and comfort them, because in my kingdom no one is left out."*

Even in life, Jesus moved toward people's exiles, toward their pain. Even when he had the power and the intention to heal the pain, he first felt *with* them.

Remember what Peter said? "Cast all your anxiety on him because he cares for you."[32]

Because he *cares*! Jesus loves us. All of us. And he invites our scared and anxious exiles to come to him so he can carry their burdens. Feel with them. Heal them.

John 11 tells an amazing story about Jesus and his *moving toward*. He was on his way to Mary and Martha's home, knowing full well that Lazarus had just died. The sisters were grief stricken, not to mention angry that Jesus had not come earlier to save Lazarus's life. Notice, however, that before Jesus lifted one finger to change the circumstances, he moved toward the sisters, their pain, and their grief. He sat *with* their grieving exiles and shared their sorrow.

> When Jesus saw her weeping, and the Jews who had come along with her also weeping, he was deeply moved in spirit and troubled. "Where have you laid him?" he asked.
>
> "Come and see, Lord," they replied. [33]

And then:
"Jesus wept."[34]
What?
Jesus wept.
Read that again.

Jesus wept.

He knew perfectly well that he would raise Lazarus from the dead. He knew with full clarity that in about five minutes, all would be well and Lazarus would be healed and the sisters' sorrow would turn to joy. In spite of that, notice Jesus's first action. His first move.

He wept.

He joined with Mary and Martha in their grief and pain, and he felt with them. He moved toward. In fact, the moving toward appears to be a precursor to the healing. Not a "Hey, quit your whining" moment, but an Immanuel moment. God *with* them in their pain.

Now, here's the amazing part. When our hurting exiles have access to our God Image, they pour out their stories and are witnessed in their pain, they receive comfort, and they can move out of their frozen state into a new place and be unburdened. When they are unburdened by the power of the God Image, they transform into something usually quite opposite of what they were before.

As we move further into our exploration of how we heal, you'll begin to experience this for yourself. While a full unburdening of an exile is beyond the scope of this book,[35] you can take the next steps toward caring compassionately for some of your exiles.

WHAT EXILES DON'T REALIZE

I want to move toward. But I have no idea what that looks like. How do I respond when an exile floods me and I feel sad, alone, afraid, rejected, or ashamed?

Great news, the answer we've known all along is right: we should respond to our exiles by running to God. But perhaps in a different way than we have previously thought.

Flood or Flooding: Flooding happens when a part takes over and completely prevents our access to the core self, or God Image. When a part floods, the individual feels its feelings, thinks its thoughts, and experiences its physical sensations. It feels as though the person *is* the part. *Flood* is the opposite of terms like *step back, unblend,* or *relax.*

Letting our exiles run to God means inviting all our burdened parts that are afraid of the exile's pain to step back and give our exile access to the divine within us: to the God Image at our core. Running to God doesn't mean allowing a Spiritualizer manager to yell at the exile and tell it not to feel, try to manage it, or to shame it. For example, "If you are feeling hurt and worried about what those people think of you, it's because you are proud. You need to humble yourself. You are doing your faith wrong. Repent of that sinful pride."

Oh, no.

The agenda-driven parts of me, which want to force me to do religious things out of shame and guilt, will have to feel comfortable enough to step back and release control before I can actually access God In Here and receive comfort and healing.

Now, it's important to know that exiles act just like hurting little children. When they are in pain and see someone (our core God Image) who can help, they run to them and try to get all of their attention, to completely take them over. So we tend to get flooded with painful exile emotions as soon as they get triggered.

How do we know if we've been flooded by an exile? Simple. We will feel as if we've been taken over by a negative emotion.

For example, I've had a number of clients who grew up with perfectionist parents. Children in these types of households often develop very young exiles that feel "not good enough." As adults, they have striving manager parts that drive them to succeed in an attempt to prove their worth. Even as highly accomplished professional adults, when these individuals encounter a situation where they perceive they've not met a standard (perhaps when the board chairman is disappointed with the company's sales numbers or when the project proposal is returned with edits), their exiles take over. They might become overwhelmed with shame and feel vulnerable and powerless, just as they did when they were young. That's what an exile does. When exiles take over, we feel like we *are* the exile. We experience the exile's emotions, thoughts, and beliefs as if they are *ours*. We say things like "I'm so ashamed" and "I'll never be good enough." Our faces flush or our posture becomes stooped.

What exiles don't realize is that our God Image can't help them if they've taken us over. They have to dial their negative emotion back a bit so we have access to God In Here before we can help. And once they figure out this is the way to get help, they do just that. You can actually tell them this—and get relief from the negative feelings.

GETTING TO KNOW AN EXILE

Some of my terminology—*flooding, stepping back, taking over*—might seem a bit strange to you, but I'm pretty sure you recognize the experience those words describe. If so, by now you're probably thinking, *I get flooded all the time with a negative emotion like shame or anxiety or fear that is way out of proportion to the situation that triggered it. And it feels awful! So what do I do to help this exile?*

Let me walk you through an exercise that may allow you to interact more effectively with your exiles. And remember, reading through a list of questions is *not* the same thing as engaging with them. That's because information doesn't change us; experience does. So take the time on each exercise and inventory in this book to engage deeply.

As you do, please go slowly and honor what comes up for you. If at any time it feels like too much, stop the exercise and take several deep breaths, go for a walk, or reach out for support. When our exiles carry substantial pain, we often need an IFS therapist to guide our experience with them. That makes complete sense. Please do whatever you need to do to take care of yourself.

Going Deeper: Getting to know an exile

When you are ready, find a quiet spot free of distractions where you can settle in comfortably. Take a couple of deep, slow breaths to communicate to your body that you are safe. Now, gently think through the following emotions, and jot a quick note to yourself about the time you can last recall feeling each emotion and the circumstance that triggered it.

- Shame
- Anxiety
- Panic
- Fear/terror
- Self-doubt
- Self-loathing
- Sadness
- Depression
- Worthlessness
- Inadequacy
- Loneliness
- Powerlessness
- Overwhelmed

Now that you've identified some of the feelings your exiles carry, choose *one* that feels reasonably mild, and let's take some time to focus on that. Please be sure to select a moderate emotion—perhaps a 2 on a scale of 0–10, where 0 is no distress and 10 is the worst distress you can imagine. (The ones that are closer to 10 will probably need more professional support the first couple of times that you interact with them in this new way.) Note the emotion, its intensity, and what triggered it.

Emotion:

Intensity (0–10):

Situation that triggered it:

Now, invite yourself to be gently present with this memory. Briefly describe the memory.

For a moment, just breathe deeply and let yourself connect with what it is like to step back into that memory. Allow the negative emotion to be present. Check and make sure all parts of you give you permission to be present with the negative emotion for a few moments.

Where (in your body) do you feel the negative emotion?

Really notice where the emotion resides in your body. You might feel a tension in your shoulders, a cold feeling in your stomach, a pain in your forehead, or tightness in your throat. Take a moment to allow your attention to be gently present with this feeling and sensation. It's okay if it escalates a little at first. When it feels safe with you, it will calm down. (You may notice a change in intensity, or the physical sensation will shift.) Welcome whatever you notice. Spend one to two minutes just being present with the sensation *with no agenda other than to notice it and be with it*.

What do you notice?

By just being present with it, did you notice any shifts?

Now, ask the part of you that is carrying this emotion if it would be willing to unblend or step back so that it is separate from you. Remind it that you can't help it with its pain until you have access to God In Here. Remember that we treat every part of ourselves with great respect. We *ask* for unblending but we never *force* (and forcing doesn't work—it usually has the reverse effect).

See what you notice and record it here:

If the emotion or sensation lessened, skip ahead to the section "When the Exile Unblends." If it did not lessen, continue here.

When the Exile Won't Unblend

If the emotion and sensations didn't shift after a minute or two, see if this part of you will share what it is afraid might happen if it unblends. It's probably afraid it won't be heard or helped. Don't worry, you won't start hearing voices! Parts communicate in a variety of ways. Some flash memories in our minds. Some give the impression of words or body sensations to reveal themselves. There is no right or wrong way to experience an exile.

Record here any sense you get about why the part is concerned about unblending:

Another option is to let the exile know what percentage of the emotion you can tolerate while still holding a strong sense of your God Image core. For example, you might say "Shame, when you flood me at 100 percent, I have no access to my spiritual core and I can't help you. I want to feel what it is like for you to carry that emotion, but I can only take about 30 percent. If you can pull back about 70 percent of that shame from me, I can get a clear sense of what it's like for you, and still bring healing power to your pain."

See what you notice and record it here:

Blend or Blending: Blending happens when a part takes over and completely obscures access to the core self, or God Image. When a part blends, the individual feels its feelings, thinks its thoughts, and experiences its physical sensations. It feels as though the person *is* the part. *Blend* is the opposite of terms like *step back*, *unblend*, *separate*, or *relax*. (Synonyms: *flood*, *take over*.)

When the Exile Unblends

If the strength of the emotion or sensation did subside, that means the exile unblended (at least partially), and you may be able to ask it to show you an image of itself in your mind's eye. Don't worry if it's a silly or weird image or even a color or a shape. There is no right or wrong way to experience a part. And yes, we often visualize parts as the opposite gender. Totally normal. No worries.

If you have a sense of what it looks like, record that here:

Do a brief Spiritual MRI or "parts check" by noticing how you feel *toward* this exile.

If you feel anything other than God Image qualities (calm, curious, compassionate, clear-minded, courageous, connected, creative, caring), you have another part blended. Probably a part that doesn't like that exile, or is afraid of the pain of that exile. Ask those feelings to step back until you feel, for example, curious or compassionate toward the exile.

It is a powerful experience for this exiled part of you to just be present with your God Image. Be with it for a moment or two. Invite it to notice you and really take in what it's like to be with you in your compassionate, spiritual core.

Going Further with an Exile

If you'd like to take this exercise a step further, ask this part of you to show you how it came to hold so much pain. It may allow various memories to pass through your mind, or it might send different sensations through your body. Remember, if the emotion of the exile starts to take you over again, simply remind it to pull back so you can be with it and help. Record what you notice.

Ask if there's anything else it wants you to know. If you get a sense of anything, write it down.

When it feels like the exile has communicated everything it needs to with you, thank it for sharing with you. Let it know you've heard it and you care about its pain.

Then gently begin to shift your attention back out into the room around you. Notice the feeling of the floor beneath your feet, and the chair or sofa supporting your body. Notice the sounds you hear in the room. Take a couple of deep breaths. You may feel a little disoriented when you first shift your attention internally. Give yourself time to adjust.

Congratulations! You have taken the first step in getting to know an exile. Take a moment and journal what this experience was like for you.

If you would like to take the next steps toward actually unburdening your exiles, you can refer to the resources section in the back of the book for tools on how to do just that. Welcome to this exciting journey of deep self-compassion and healing!

Discussion Questions

- What did you learn from this chapter about the value of pain?

- What thoughts come up when you consider the statement, "If you can't feel pain, you don't know when something is wrong"? What would it look like for you to listen well to your pain?

- Do you connect with any of the common strategies we use to avoid feeling our pain? How have they worked for you in the short run? In the long run?

- Out of the list of ways that exiles develop, which ones connect for you?

- Why do you think exiles that develop covertly (for example, from overly high expectations, rather than abuse or abandonment) are hard to recognize and validate?

- What is one exile part within you that you can recognize as carrying pain? How did it develop?

- When you think about the pain your exiles carry, what is it like for you to consider the reality that "Jesus wept" and was *with* Mary and Martha in their pain?

- If you are aware of any of your exiles, what kind of comfort do you think they might need?

5

MEETING OUR MANAGERS

Parts that work hard to *prevent* pain

I grew up in a military family, and moving around all the time didn't exactly create an environment conducive to having pets. So, I was determined that when I grew up and became Master of My Own Domain, I was absolutely going to have pets. Yes, that's plural. I had a lot to make up for. But it wasn't until after I married and had a couple of kids that I finally got serious about a trip to the animal shelter.

That's where we found our Shih Tzu—it's pronounced *shee-tzu*, thank you very much—named Bella. Bella had been rescued from a puppy mill, and she was *perfect*. She needed us as much as we needed her.

Some parts of Bella's early life never left her. She was terrified of thunderstorms and loud noises. Plus, things that floated in the air. Goodness knows what that was about.

Bella never could walk very far, and in her later years, she was pretty much blind and deaf and slept most of the time. Bella wouldn't—okay, couldn't—hurt anything, but we were her people and she was determined to do everything she could to keep us safe.

One seemingly innocent day, a Winnie the Pooh balloon came into our home, attached to a birthday present for one of my kids. Alarmed at the intrusion, Bella sprang into blind Shih Tzu–ninja action to alert us to the danger threatening our safety. She bravely took up her battle station, standing as close to Winnie as she could, and barked without ceasing until we were fully alerted to the peril and placed the balloon in a closet where she could no longer see it.

With fear and trembling, she was determined to help us with that terrifying, life-threatening situation. Which, of course, wasn't actually terrifying or life threatening at all. But it probably was for her at one time, way back in the puppy mill when she was locked in a too-small crate and powerless to get out or change her circumstances.

Do you know a cool thing about courage? It doesn't require actual danger; it only requires fear. Fear . . . and the *perception* of danger.

Without fear, we can't be courageous. Even if what we're facing isn't dangerous, and what we are doing isn't helpful.

This is exactly what our protectors do. These parts of us see situations that appear to be scary—that probably actually *were* scary in the past—and try to help with the fear or pain or anxiety or loneliness or whatever the unhealed exiles inside us happen to be feeling in the moment. They try, and keep on trying, even when what they're doing doesn't work or isn't needed anymore.

That's why they are called protectors. Because they try to protect us from the pain. Just like Bella, they are so courageous! Well intentioned. And completely unaware when they aren't helping at all.

We've seen that pain from past trauma and negative life experiences lives on in our exiles, and how those hurting parts trigger other parts to spring into action. In this chapter we introduce a whole lineup of highly motivated protector parts. Many you'll recognize. I'm guessing you'll meet at least one you know inside and out.

If you're like me, you might even meet one you've always thought was the actual, whole, forever, *real* you.

I promise you'll come away not just with helpful understanding of your bravest protector parts, but also with a new appreciation for why they're trying so hard to save you from all that threatens.

TWO OF A KIND

We all have two very different types of protectors: managers and firefight-ers. They have the same goal (helping with pain) but take completely opposite approaches. Managers are the *proactive* team; they work hard attempting to *prevent* pain. Firefighters are *reactive*. They try to "put out" pain when it shows up. Both are afraid of the pain of the exiles, and both unintentionally make it worse.

Manager: A burdened protector part that attempts to manage or control events proactively, to prevent the pain of exile(s) from being activated. Common manager strategies include controlling, people pleasing, striving, judging, self-criticizing, and attempting to do things perfectly.

People dominated by managers tend to congregate in churches, gyms, and PTAs. People dominated by firefighters tend to congregate in bars and Las Vegas. Makes no difference: they are both good types of parts, trying to help. They are just stuck in bad roles.

Oh, and one last thing: Managers and firefighters often hate each other. Much of our internal and external pain comes from the intensity of their battles.

Firefighter: A burdened protector part that attempts to extinguish the pain of exile(s) reactively, after it has been triggered. Common firefighter strategies include addictions, eating, self-harm, violence, dissociation, obsession, compulsion, fantasy, rage.

When the exiles these parts protect gain access to our God Image core and are healed, protectors no longer need to do their unhelpful jobs. They, too, can be unburdened and freed up to do more helpful things, things they were created to do. Most of our healing comes from the releasing of the protectors' and exiles' burdens.

When we understand that protectors serve important roles, we can stop our ineffective strategies for dealing with them.

Remember our "Stop it" strategy? Yeah. If we only try to force protectors to stop their behavior (e.g., drinking, raging, controlling, overworking, people pleasing), we are ignoring the pain of the exiles that are driving the behavior. This type of *move against* approach will ultimately be ineffective. Any stopping that happens will be temporary. It's just white knuckling because the pain underneath is still unaddressed.

Addiction counselors know that white knuckling is not sobriety; it is a precursor to relapse. But healing the deeper exiles and honoring the goal the protectors are trying to accomplish give us far more effective ways of changing unwanted behaviors.

Here and in the next chapter, we'll get to know the managers and learn how to relate to them in more helpful ways.

MANAGERS, THE PROACTIVE TEAM

Our manager parts are often *luuuuuved* by our families, friends, bosses, co-workers, faith communities, and the lady who has to organize volunteers for the Sunday school program.

These parts generally work hard, look good, meet deadlines, and make up for the guy in the back who didn't quite get his part of the proposal finished for the group presentation. They are a pretty exhausted bunch, but they're always prepared to spring into action at a moment's notice. Remember, these proactive managers are trying to prevent rejection and pain by doing, pleasing, and performing.

> Managers are trying to prevent rejection and pain by doing, pleasing, and performing.

It's probably most practical to introduce you to the managers by some of the behaviors they get stuck in. Managers are much more complex than just these behaviors, and there are more than included here, but this will give you a general sense of what they're like.

Do you recognize any parts of you in the following?

PERFECTIONIST

Those of us who are only children or firstborns or grew up in environments with high standards or competition tend to develop these kinds of manager strategies. Get it right, do it right—every time.

Guilty. This is one of mine.

This manager usually protects the exile with the burden of "not good enough." The Perfectionist part thinks that if it can do everything perfectly, then people will like us and tell us how great we are and then we will feel good enough.

There's one small problem. If this part makes even one tiny mistake, it tumbles into the pit of despair and gets flooded by all the "not good enough" pain. It's a pretty brutal task manager. It does turn in an A-plus term paper or work proposal. And all the *attaboys* it earns do feel pretty good. For a minute.

But that does not help us to be real and to be seen in relationships, which is what ultimately helps to heal all the painful "not good enough" stuff it's protecting.

When Perfectionist is in charge, we will intimidate others who think they can't measure up to us. (Their "less than" exiles are activated by our Perfectionist manager, which is protecting our "less than" exiles). Then they wear a mask to match our mask, and we don't have real relationships, which makes us feel not good enough . . . and then our exiles get stronger . . . and then . . . well, you get the picture.

Perfectionist has another problem: when it does perform perfectly and receive the applause, all the praise goes to the perfectionist mask. No matter how much praise and affirmation is earned, it can't sink in, because none of it is going to the real, flawed person underneath. So the Perfectionist part spins and spins to "do it right," feeding off the scraps of good feelings that come with momentary praise and success, only to feel worse because the exile's core belief of, "If you knew the real, flawed me, you wouldn't love me," is still every bit as powerful as before. It's an exhausting, depleting circle of futility.

DOER

Doer keeps us moving so fast and working so hard that we can't feel our feelings. Or our bodies. Or really anything at all. Except maybe stress and anxiety. But that's a lot better than feeling the pain it's keeping numbed, so it doesn't mind the chaos—especially because the stress makes us race through life even faster and with more chaos. Doer's goal is to keep us in a state of overwhelm so that there is no time to feel.

Because the feelings that bubble up when Doer gets still are unpleasant, uncomfortable, and scary.

This manager has a to-do list that rarely gets completely checked off, and on the one or two days that every item is checked off, Doer feels anxious rather than relieved, because it hates to be still. Stillness is scary.

People with this manager overvolunteer, overwork, overtravel, over-entertain, and sign their kids up for sports and music lessons and Latin clubs to keep themselves busy driving their kids to all these places. Doer does not consciously realize it is choosing chaos, yet it gravitates toward intensity and whirlwind, often because that's what felt normal in the environment where Doer was raised. Addiction, abuse, divorce, and perfectionism are common themes in Doer's early life, and Doer unconsciously re-creates that chaos through overcommitment and the motto, "When I just get through this season of life, then I can relax."

This manager is glorified in our competitive culture, so our Doer managers are often the ones we lead with in conversation.

"Hey, great to see you! How are you and the kids?"

"Great to see you too! We are busy, really busy. Sally plays three sports, and Johnny is taking eight AP classes, and I run the PTA and teach Bible study. We are so busy. Good, but busy. How about you guys?"

"Yeah, we're busy, too. Pablo is president of his student body and on the travel baseball team, so we are out of town every weekend with games, and Hector travels every week for work, and I teach barre five mornings a week and then commute an hour to work. We are busy. Super busy. But good."

"We should get together sometime."

The problem is, a Doer manager moves so fast, it prevents us from listening to the exhaustion and resentment that are telling us we are over-extended. At some point, our bodies can't hold up under the pace, so we get irritable bowel syndrome or adrenal fatigue or thyroid malfunction or high blood pressure or the flu or throw our backs out and there we go, stopped short right in the middle of our lives. And now Doer is completely out of options to keep the pain at bay.

We get flooded with the pain *and* we have irritable bowels. Yikes.

THINKER

A Thinker manager is often smart. It figures things out. And it knows lots of stuff. It consumes information, head knowledge, data, and facts. People with Thinker managers often rise to the tops of their fields, write amazing dissertations, and make terrific contributions on Q&A panels. Thinker is easy to confuse with sheer intellect. But we know the difference because Thinker will keep us confined to our thoughts and out of our hearts. Because just like Doer, Thinker's job is to prevent us from feeling.

A Thinker manager effectively guillotines the head from the heart and body, and it strands the person they are protecting at the emotional age when the Thinker developed. Thinker hides a five-year-old emotional being behind a forty-year-old intellectual being. And that gets pretty confusing when feelings have to be felt.

People who have survived pain by developing a Thinker come into my office and tell me the most horrific stories of suffering with no emotion or expression. They respond "good" or "fine" when I ask them how they feel. I gently remind them that "good" and "fine" are not emotions, so they say "tired" or "overwhelmed." I gently remind them that those are physical states of being and not emotions, and they look at me in utter confusion. They cannot finish the sentence "I feel _____" with a feeling word (such as *vulnerable, powerful, afraid, lonely, elated, resentful, numb,* or *skeptical*) because Thinkers do not have an emotional vocabulary and are expressly forbidden to connect with the heart. If they did that, they fear they might not be able to hold back the tide of grief or desperation or shame that awaits.

As smart and thoughtful as Thinkers are, they are very effective at avoiding feeling. Especially difficult feelings. That's because trauma shatters our core selves and separates our heads from our hearts from our bodies. So, if you have experienced negative circumstances, you're likely to minimize or rationalize your pain. You'll say, "The sexual abuse was my fault," or "The divorce wasn't that bad," because you have parts preventing you from feeling how bad it really was. That's why our bodies often carry so much pain and illness: they are trying to get the attention of our heads to notice the pain that is stuffed so tightly into our hearts. That's also why learning what we are feeling and being present to what we are experiencing in our bodies is such a key part of healing. We are reintegrating our shattered selves.

CONTROLLER

Controller is a manager intent on creating safety. It often hides the pain of an exile that experienced powerlessness or a lack of safety at a key developmental point. Controller strives to manage people and circumstances so that the out-of-control or frightening things it has experienced will never happen again. Unfortunately, by working so hard to control others, it unintentionally communicates "You do not have what it takes to manage your life. Be more like me, and you will be better." Which evokes the very rejection and distancing it is trying to avoid.

Controller's motto is, "God has a wonderful plan for your life, and I know what it is." It has an agenda for others and is upset when others do not welcome or accept its uninvited advice and high-pressure tactics. It isn't able to consider that other people experience the world differently than it does, and that people might have different thoughts, feelings, desires, and preferences. It directs its attention outward, toward what others are doing, in part to avoid having to look inward, at the uncomfortable realities of its inner experience.

People with this manager sometimes congregate in communities that feel they have the right answers that need to be imposed on others—for example, some faith communities, political parties, and economically or socially privileged environments. We know this manager is in place—contrasted with a healthy, unburdened part that is settled in its understanding of truth and warmly invites others to dialogue about it—when there is fear, anxiety, or a forceful agenda underneath its interest in changing others.

The exile behind Controller is usually quite small and scared and very much in need of the safety and predictability that Controller is attempting to create. Strong Controller managers often indicate the presence of terrified exiles.

PASSIVE

Passive is an interesting manager strategy. It has a relaxed and neutral countenance to go with a safety-oriented line of reasoning: "Just don't try. Don't take initiative. Don't believe you can. Don't make any effort. Don't step out of the comfort zone. Don't make waves. It's not worth it and probably won't work out, so don't even go there." Passive managers often believe that if you don't try, you can't fail, and therefore can't get hurt.

People dominated by this manager sit on the couch a lot. They don't go to the gym, interview for the promotion, ask their spouse on a date night, initiate ball throwing with the kids in the backyard, or engage in conflict of any kind.

A Passive manager shuts things down and removes people from actually experiencing their lives. In a way, it makes them nonpeople, which can be maddening to relate to if you are a person who is dominated by a high-performing pack of Perfectionist or Controller managers.

Passive strategies are often trying to protect the pain of the exile who feels worthless, uncared for, powerless, and victimized. Passive managers are often working hard to keep us small so that we do not risk the world's judgment and rejection. And they are often oblivious to the fact that their passivity is actually inviting the very judgment and rejection that they fear most.

SELF-SABOTAGER

A Passive manager has an interesting variation that can show up in driven and accomplished people: the Self-Sabotager. This manager allows the person to achieve to the level of joy, love, or success it feels the person deserves, and then it pulls a switch, creating all manner of ways to distract, derail, or devalue any additional achievement.

Sound irrational? Not at all. A Self-Sabotager manager says, "Who are you to do that big thing? You shouldn't set your sights on unrealistic stuff, so just stay here in this comfortable, smaller place. You have everything you need here, and if you risk it, you might find out you really don't deserve it."

Self-Sabotager strategies operate in similar ways to Passive strategies; they just tend to kick in later and have a higher tolerance for success. The goal is to keep us small so that we don't have to face potential rejection from the world, or the pain of failure.

PESSIMIST

Pessimist managers frequently hang out with Passive managers, and they watch a lot of football sitting on the couch.

Pessimist is the Eeyore of managers, because it has something negative to say about everything. It's certain the end of the world is upon us, the government is hopeless and filled with a bunch of liars, the teacher is biased and doesn't know what she's doing, the boss is a micromanager and just cares about his big office, the spouse is a nag, the kids are failures, the girlfriend/boyfriend is needy, and the guy at the gas station who pulled in front of you to fill up really had it out for you.

Pessimist is into global words like *always* and *never.* ("You *always* treat me like manure." "You *never* care what I want.")

You are catching on, aren't you? You know why Pessimist is a manager, right? If Pessimist can keep you thinking the worst of everything and everyone, then you won't be disappointed when other people are . . . human.

Ahhh.

Of course, in its efforts to avoid disappointment, Pessimist is actually creating disappointment, but usually without realizing it. Pessimist strategies are often trying to protect exiles that feel hopeless, powerless, and worthless.

Isn't it amazing how every one of our manager strategies actually creates the very thing (pain) that they are trying to avoid? Every manager truly means well but is stuck doing things out of fear of pain that limit our flexibility and authenticity.

The seven we've met so far are so common that you can probably identify with several. We have three more to go—and they're biggies. I take more time to explore our next manager here because in both my personal and professional experience, it seems to burden people of faith the minute we earn our first gold sticker in Sunday school.

PLEASER/SERVER

The people Pleaser/Server looks really, really good on the outside, and it feels for all the world like it is driven by love. In fact, most people who are dominated by this manager think that self-ignoring serving *is* love.

The idea that authentic love involves giving *and* receiving makes this manager really uncomfortable, because it doesn't like to receive. It doesn't feel worthy of receiving.

By working so hard to be invaluable, Pleaser/Server hopes that it will be needed, appreciated, and liked. The exile it is working so hard to protect often feels unseen, unappreciated, or worthless, and it courts exhaustion trying to fix that pain.

Pleaser/Server chronically ignores its own feelings and needs while it focuses on taking care of everyone else's feelings and needs. This manager is dependent upon other people liking it to feel worthy. As a result, it is so others-focused and so effectively cut off from authentic Self that people with strong Pleaser/Server have no idea what they feel, need, or want. It is truly Self-less, with no sense of Self. Which is one of those crazy things that sounds really good until you realize it really isn't.

Funny—well, not really funny at all, but at least good to know—that certain managers and firefighters seem made for each other. That is, their coping strategies fit together. For example, Pleasers makes a great fit with firefighters who drink, abuse, or act out sexually, because both agree the pleaser's feelings don't matter. So Pleaser and Drinker marry and wind up in our offices in a lot of pain.

More than anything, Pleaser/Server needs others to be happy with it so that it feels loved. And wanted. And needed. So that it has a place and a reason to exist.

Pleaser will say yes when it means no. It will go to a Chinese restaurant because its friend wants Chinese, even though it prefers pizza. It will serve everyone else's dinner and drinks and will forget to eat or even sit down.

Notice the huge difference between Pleaser/Server and an authentic, servant-hearted part serving out of an overflowing heart with no agenda or need for appreciation. That authentic type of part would be unburdened and helpful.

Christlike, even.

In my experience, people who come of age in churches often struggle with a Pleaser/Server burden. That's why I want to look closely at some familiar scriptures to see what we might have gotten confused about this part.

Jesus famously encountered Pleaser/Server in his beloved friend Martha as she frantically prepared for company. I don't know about you, but as a kid who grew up in a military family that entertained constantly, I can so relate to Martha's experience. I feel a little protective of her.

Watching her scurry around before dinner one day, Jesus said to her, "Martha, Martha, you are worried and upset about many things."[36]

Hang on, Jesus. That seems really unfair. I mean, somebody *had to* make dinner if you were gonna eat. It's not like they had the Domino's app on their phone, and Mary and the guys sure weren't cooking.*

While we're on the subject, don't our churches teach that we are supposed to self-sacrificially serve others? That we should think of others' needs before our own? Isn't thinking about our own feelings and needs selfish, narcissistic, and ungodly? Isn't there some priority list that says our value system should be: 1. God, 2. others, and 3. self?

Our confusion over this manager is an honest one. Let's take a closer look. What does the Bible say about this?

In Galatians 6:2, Paul teaches, "Carry each other's burdens, and in this way you will fulfill the law of Christ."

But wait, right after that—I mean *right* after that—the apostle says, "for each one should carry their own load."[37]

Which one is it? Anyone else confused?

I have to confess, I have a nerdy-academic part that loves knowing about the Greek and Hebrew, so when the English doesn't make sense, I can't resist checking those out. A wonderful Bible teacher that I know opened my eyes to this truth.[38]

Turns out *burden*—don't you love that scripture keeps calling these *burdens*?—is *bare* in Greek, and means an overwhelming weight or sorrow or grief, something bigger than one person can carry. *Load* in the Greek is *phortion,* which is like a backpack—just what each person needs to provide for their own needs. It is personal and, by definition, not transferable.

So, if my neighbor encounters a burden like cancer or divorce or infertility or loss of a child, I can, out of an authentic overflow of my heart, come alongside her and help care for her pain and needs. But in the daily responsibilities of life, if I do for someone what they can and should do for themselves—especially if I'm doing it so they will like me and see me as a good person—I just stepped out of my biblical mandate and into Pleaser/Server.

In fairness, it's easy to get those two guys confused if you don't speak Greek.

And then there's, "Love the Lord your God with all your heart and with all your soul and with all your mind and with all your strength. . . . Love your neighbor as yourself."[39]

There. Jesus said "Love your neighbor as yourself" was the second greatest commandment.

John records it even more succinctly: "My command is this: Love each other as I have loved you."[40]

And he repeats it for emphasis a few verses later: "This is my command: Love each other."[41]

Period. That's it. The big Mac Daddy. The one-sentence CliffsNotes for my whole, huge, multipound Bible that I drag around occasionally to those churches where it doesn't look holy enough for me to look up the scripture on my phone. Because they might think I was texting.

If all the law and all the prophets hang on this pithy sentence, shouldn't we take a moment to deconstruct it?

Where do we start? Love God. We've established the best way I can do that is to invite all my parts to unblend, which allows me to fully experience God in me and his love planted firmly in the depths of my being from the beginning of time.

Got it. Next?

Love my neighbor . . . as myself.

It looks like loving the neighbor comes second after loving God and before loving self. But wait—is that really right?

There's a prerequisite. I have to love myself first if I am going to love my neighbor as I love myself. If I don't love myself, then loving my neighbor that way would mean *not* loving my neighbor. I'm not God or anything, but I'm pretty sure that's not what he meant.

> If I don't love myself, then loving my neighbor that way would mean not loving my neighbor.

Are you saying loving myself is a mandatory prerequisite to loving others? So if I'm "serving" my "neighbor" out of a burdened attempt to gain approval and sense of worth and am completely depleted in the process, this is not godly?

I believe that's exactly what the text says.

So I have to love myself—which means knowing and honoring what I think, need, and feel—before I can be freed to appropriately serve others? And the corollary to that is that if I am serving others to my detriment and without first knowing and honoring what I need, want, and feel, I am actually not being biblical?

Yes, serving is good. Yes, caring for others is good. Serving sacrificially is good. But not out of Pleaser/Server. Not with an agenda. Not with a need to be good enough or to gain approval, or out of shame or guilt. Only out of an overflow of the direct, guiltless, agendaless leading of the God Image within us.

TOWARD COMPASSION FOR HELPERS

All burdened protectors are trying to help us with our pain. That includes the manager part that gets you a raise (Perfectionist, Doer, or Pleaser/Server) and the ones that might get you left out (Controller, Pessimist, Self-Sabotager).

In the next chapter we meet two more managers, and I'll demonstrate a practical six-step approach to bringing them compassion and assistance. The outcome for you will be a lot more clarity, calm, and compassion in your life.

Discussion Questions

- You met a whole lineup of managers in this chapter who try to protect us from pain: Perfectionist, Doer, Thinker, Controller, Passive, Self-Sabotager, Pessimist, and Pleaser/Server. Which ones can you most identify with, and why?

- If you are a person of faith, which manager would you say feels most wrapped up in your understanding of scripture or your experience in church?

- If you've ever experienced a tension between serving others and honoring yourself, how might understanding Pleaser/Server help?

6

RELIEF FOR
OUR MANAGERS

Two major managers &
the Six Fs in action

I've saved this chapter for two of our hardest working managers who also tend to create the most confusion in our inner and outer worlds. They deserve additional space, understanding, and compassion as they strive so diligently to get us to "do it right."

To help you encounter these parts in action, we'll walk through a hypothetical conversation between a therapist and a client who feels stuck relating to a painful manager. And I'll show you how to apply the powerful Six Fs to your own life.

Now that we understand many of the parts of our inner worlds, we can start to put them together in a way that we've probably never imagined before.

CRITIC/JUDGE

In our competitive, individualistic, performance- and appearance-oriented America, I have never encountered anyone who did not at least occasionally deal with this manager's tactics. It's so familiar that you could probably write its job description.

We often experience a Critic/Judge manager as nasty and mean spirited. When it's turned outward, it's the Judge. When it's turned inward, it's the Critic. Either way, it engages in a constant narrative of faults, imperfections, and shortcomings, and magnifies them until it seems there is nothing left but the flaw.

A Critic/Judge shows itself in several intonations and attitudes. One is the mean-girl teenage voice that has its hand on its hip and rolls its eyes and tips its nose up just a bit. One is the clipboard-holding, magnifying glass–wielding inspector that zeroes in on any real or perceived flaw and magnifies it. Another is the angry-parent type that yells and shames and pushes its agenda of appearance, performance, or perfection. If we happened to have that kind of parent, we may come to believe it is God's voice too.

I promise that's not God. Far from it.

Our media, by the way, does not help with this, because it piles on to our Critic/Judge parts. Yes, this happens in impossibly perfect images from advertising and movies and shows. We are familiar with its tactics. We've all seen the voyeuristic "entertainment" where people's every flaw and shortcoming are highlighted as they are voted off the island / the ropes course / the cooking show / the runway / the stage one by one until only The Best remains. And no one else counts. Everyone else is a loser.

Our Judges relish the scrutiny of others' flaws while our Critics amp up the volume in our own heads.

Wait—you're saying Critics and Judges are managers? I thought managers were supposed to prevent pain, not cause it. Somebody must have put this one in the wrong category.

Well, I understand the confusion, but remember I didn't say these managers were *effective* at making pain go away. (In the long run, none of them are.) I said they were *trying*. Unfortunately, they're often oblivious to the pain they are causing.

The Critic zeroes in on how fat you are, or how could you have said that dumb thing last night, or how stupid you are that you forgot that appointment, or how undesirable you are that no one will ever go out with you, or how hopeless you are that you'll never amount to anything.

Yes, those critical narratives are painful, but they do keep us "small" and scare us into "doing it right." According to the Critic, that is exactly the point.

Critic wants me to believe I'm too fat or too ugly or too stupid to get out in the world and try; that way it can minimize the amount I hear those things from others. Not to mention that Critic believes if it yells at me enough, then I won't mess up or do it wrong. It wants to protect me from failing, from being rejected and disappointed.

The Judge, on the other hand, zeroes in on how fat or stupid or lazy or less-than or hopeless that other person (or people group, political party, religion, gender, or race) is, because if it can keep us focused on those other people's flaws, we won't have to look at our own. If we still stumble over our own flaws, at least we aren't as bad as those people or that group. It's the one-up strategy for trying to hide our shame.

The Judge/Critic is often trying to help the pain of exiles who feel broken, worthless, unchosen, undesirable, or not included. Of course, by engaging in these hurtful views and narratives, these managers make the pain worse and in fact *create* this exiled pain in others.

But these parts usually don't see that. They are working hard to try to help. Like so many other managers, they are tireless and well-intentioned.

SPIRITUALIZER

This is a tough one. If part of you is feeling defensive at the very name, please know this is a hard-working, well-intentioned part. Just like any other manager. Yet in its efforts to be stay spiritually true, Spiritualizer is actually keeping us away from an authentic experience of God. It doesn't realize that, of course. It's fully persuaded that it is righteous and pursuing holiness.

Let's get to know Spirititualizer and see if it's a familiar friend.

The Spiritualizer's coping strategy is often a religious twist on other manager strategies, Perfectionist, Doer, Controller, Critic/Judge, and Pleaser/Server among them. It often comes into being because people who are dominated by these managers become Christians or get involved in church.

Of course, wanting to know, say, and do the right things is not bad, and wanting to do those things for God is not bad either. The challenge comes when Spiritualizer striving takes over an authentic faith journey in an attempt to *earn* righteousness, God's approval, or the church's approval. Or to protect an exile that feels unworthy, broken, or unseen.

A Spiritualizer manager will do, say, and think spiritual things. It will go to church, teach Sunday school, volunteer at VBS, tithe, teach Bible study, witness to neighbors, go on mission trips, and otherwise *do* many good and churchy things. It also will speak with spiritual language, pray with impressive churchy words, and talk about sin, redemption, and Jesus.

This is a stealth manager strategy because on the surface, it looks a lot like true spirituality (which comes from our core God Image when all our parts—especially our Spiritualizer parts—have stepped back). But there are some dead giveaways, and you probably know what they are because you've sat across from them at some point. You recognize the reflexive response inside you: hide, pretend, cover up, say something churchy, force yourself to be something you are not, judge or be judged.

Unlike our authentic spiritual essence, which is compassionate, curious, and filled with genuine love for the person with whom it is speaking, Spiritualizer will have an agenda for you (Do It Right/Controller), impossible standards (Perfectionist), and a thinly veiled spirit of "righteous" judgment and shaming (Critic/Judge). It will be uncomfortable with messy human experience or negative emotions. And that makes perfect sense because the whole job of a burdened part is to avoid messy human experience and negative emotion. This manager just does it with spiritual language.

Unlike receiving prayer from someone's God Image core, which creates safety, intimacy, and care, we often feel vulnerable or exposed when prayed for by a Spiritualizer part. This type of prayer may feel like a disguised evaluation of our spiritual performance.

"God, please don't let Joe here feel afraid/ashamed/anxious."(Because I— Spiritualizer—avoid negative emotions, they are bad.)

"I cast out that sin in the name of Jesus." (You are in sin; I am not.)

"Protect him from pride." (I'm evaluating you as either proud or at risk of being proud.)

"Help him to see you clearly." (You are not seeing God clearly, and you need to get your spiritual focus en pointe *here, buddy.)*

Spiritualizer, because it actually inhibits an authentic experience with God, will do its best to emulate what it thinks God should do, and winds up making God into the image of man. It sincerely believes God can't handle our negative feelings or messy behaviors and struggles. Just like it can't, because remember, the whole point of a manager strategy is to avoid pain.

Spiritualizer will work very, very hard at spiritual activities like prayer or Bible study or volunteering or evangelism and then get burned out and disillusioned when it gets exhausted and isn't feeling that connection with God it so strongly desires. But it can't say that out loud, because it's not allowed to admit imperfection.

Spiritualizer will teach that if you feel fear or depression or anxiety or stress, if you have mental health issues or if you struggle with certain behaviors, you are not right with God. It will provide you with a list of ten scriptures showing why you are not in line with biblical teaching. It will advise, "If you struggle with X or Y, you need to do this spiritual activity instead and shape up." It has lots of strategies for what you need to do or not do to become more acceptable, less messy, and less real. Spiritualizer is focused on a standard, on behaviors and judgment. Sadly, all the while it moves further and further from an authentic experience of God. From love. Which is the very essence of the God that it is trying so hard to please.

If I listen to someone who is speaking from their God Image talk about fear, anxiety, shame, or loneliness, I will hear a spirit of compassion, grace, and empathy. A *moving toward.* Just like Jesus did. No agenda. No shame. That's why people who felt all those painful things and felt judged by the (Spiritualizer) Pharisees came flocking to Jesus.

However, if I listen to someone who is speaking from Spiritualizer talk about fear, anxiety, or loneliness, my parts will get activated. My exiles may feel *more* shame and need to hide. I may feel judged and unwelcome. I may feel like I'm not doing it right and that my faith is not as good as that Spiritualizer person's faith.

I can tell it's a part, and not the God Image, because it has an agenda, it is shaming, it is judging, and my parts react. Same goes for conversations about money, relationships, parenting, sex, and volunteering.

Yes, but what about truth? What about showing people the error of their sinful ways? What about pointing people to God?

Jesus had a way of holding clearly and nondefensively to his truth, of living with such compassion that people's defended parts felt safe to step back—and they journeyed to their own internal conviction/repentance. Jesus directed people to God by his grace-filled, compassionate presence. The reality Jesus knew and lived out is that truth and conviction are *not* most effectively communicated by confrontation, judgment, and shame, but rather by love, compassion, and connection.

Jesus himself was deeply saddened and had clear words for the Spiritualizing parts of the church leaders of his day:

> "Woe to you, teachers of the law and Pharisees, you hypocrites! You are like whitewashed tombs, which look beautiful on the outside but on the inside are full of the bones of the dead and everything unclean. In the same way, on the outside you appear to people as righteous but on the inside you are full of hypocrisy and wickedness."[42]

If this is how Jesus felt about Spiritualizer—stronger words than he used with most any other sin—I think I'd better sit up and pay attention.

It's a bit of a dilemma because when we are overtaken by a Spiritualizer part we don't realize it, and we're apt to be quite strongly defended against that possibility. The Pharisees had absolutely no idea they weren't the perfect models of spirituality. And they weren't very open to considering a different opinion.

Of course they weren't. Our burdened parts are defended by their very nature. One easy litmus test to see if we are in our authentic God Image core or a Spiritualizer part is to see how we feel about examining our own actions and motivations. If we feel defensive, we are in a part. If we feel open and curious, chances are good we are in our authentic God Image within.

Have you ever noticed that many people associate the word *hate* with Christians?

Something is really off, because Jesus pretty clearly said, "By this everyone will know that you are my disciples, if you love one another."[43] Why do many people experience Christians as the exact *opposite* of what Christ told us to be?

When I understand Spiritualizer, this suddenly makes sense. It's simply the difference between authentic spirituality and Spiritualizer parts. My parts have nothing to react to in someone responding out of their God Image, because no burdened parts are present. When we are in our authentic spiritual core, others experience truth blended with grace and compassion.

You might have had the joy of sitting under the teaching of someone speaking from their God Image, perhaps a gifted pastor, Bible study leader, or friend. This person could communicate spiritual truths and biblical exhortations in a way that was invitational—that called you to something wonderfully higher without shaming or judging or pressuring. That's authentic spirituality. Winsome. Grace with truth. It was a *move toward* kind of experience. You felt safe and wanted more. You were attracted to their way of life and their teaching.

Spiritualizer will unfortunately have the reverse effect. Even when it uses really, really similar words. It leaves us feeling judged, defeated, isolated, broken, ashamed, not good enough, and hopeless. We will want to hide.

Please remember, our Spiritualizer parts are well-meaning. They are sincerely trying to do what they think is right, and they have absolutely no idea they are not being Christlike. They are trying really hard to earn God's and others' favor and to protect vulnerable little exiles that believe they are broken, unwanted, or not enough. And it's pretty scary to fear that you are not good enough for God, so Spiritualizer has to be very strong. As with most protectors, we often inherited this manager from our parents or our childhood faith communities, so looking honestly at it may even feel disloyal. And that's hard. I'm so glad we have the courage and the curiosity to explore this together. I know it's uncomfortable. But enlightening too, no?

We sure serve a surprising God, and a loving one. Thank goodness.

NO BAD PARTS, ONLY BAD ROLES

Now that you've had a chance to get familiar with a few of these manager strategies, you may understand in a fresh way how amazing these hard-working parts of you are. You may have a deep awareness of the pain they are trying to help you avoid. This is a good time to highlight again a really important concept: there are no bad parts, only bad roles. All burdened protectors are trying to help us with our pain. Even when they're doing it in unhelpful ways.

That's so critical to remember, because when we are introduced to parts whose behaviors aren't helpful, our other parts may get activated about it. For example, when we discover that the Spiritualizer part we thought was faith is actually keeping us *away* from God, a part of us—probably the Perfectionist part—will immediately want to know how to kick that no-good Spiritualizer off the team. That's because it's normal for our parts to be at war.

While that instinct may seem virtuous, the get-rid-of-it sentiment isn't an expression of our God Image. It's just a part getting a little over-heated. Our essential core is compassionate and openhearted toward every last one of our parts. Any anger we feel toward our Spiritualizer is something that needs witnessing and unburdening every bit as much as the spiritualizing.

UNBURDENED PARTS

While we're at it, let's remember that not all parts are stuck in extreme roles. We have some parts that are not burdened and have flexibility in their behavior and choices. These are good and helpful, because here in this season between Eden and heaven, it is not possible to walk around in God Image all the time.

Our various unburdened parts show up to help us move through the world in unique and beautiful ways. These unburdened parts make up what we call our personalities; they make us who we uniquely are.

For example, my son has a car part. I mean, this boy loves cars. He knows everything about every car ever made and can rattle off model numbers faster than I can count. He can tell you what kind of super cool car is about to pass us without having to lay eyes on it because he can tell by hearing its engine.

This is his fun and joyful car part. It is just who he uniquely is. It's not burdened, not protecting an exile, not serving any role other than to make him a fabulously interesting person to talk to about vehicular transportation. And keep him utterly mystified at his mom, who thinks cars are simply devices to get you from point A to point B, with the best safety and gas mileage possible, please.

That one is pretty clear. Fun car part. But sometimes burdened and unburdened parts look really similar on the surface. How do we know which is which?

Easy—we look underneath. What's driving the behavior? An exile? A fear? A need? Burdened parts are trying to protect us from pain. Unburdened parts aren't.

For example, if we have a burdened manager coping with Perfectionist strategies, then it must "do it right" or it will be awash in exile shame and self-condemnation. It's stuck in the role of doing things perfectly.

> *Burdened parts are trying to protect us from pain. Unburdened parts aren't.*

That's very different than a do-it-well part that is not burdened (stuck in extreme behavior) and likes to do things well because that shows honor and care for the work. It's not protecting an exile, so doing things well is not a life-or-death proposition for this part.

An unburdened do-it-well part might make a mistake, shrug its shoulders, learn from the mistake, and carry on with minimal distraction. The behavior of the burdened perfectionist and unburdened do-it-well part look similar on the surface—they both try to do work well—but serve different functions internally. One hides an exile; the other doesn't. The ones hiding exiles are the ones we want to unburden.

BRINGING FORWARD ANNA'S CRITIC

Now that you are familiar with some of the more common manager strategies, you'd probably like to meet a few of your own. But before I take you through an exercise to help you experience your own managers, perhaps it would be helpful to listen in on someone else meeting theirs. After all, this is a really different way of relating to ourselves. It takes a while to figure out what it looks like.

Anna is a fictitious client that is representative of a typical "parts" session in counseling. Notice that, when meetings parts, it's often helpful to use the "Six F" principles which I will explain further in a moment: (1) Find, (2) Focus, (3) Flesh Out, (4) Feel, (5) BeFriend, and (6) Fear. For now, just notice how the therapist uses the Six Fs in this session, and then I'll walk you through a Six F exercise so you can try it for yourself.

Six Fs: An IFS technique for getting to know a part:
(1) Find, (2) Focus, (3) Flesh Out, (4) Feel, (5) BeFriend, and (6) Fear.

Let's say Anna is a forty-five-year-old professional female who is a successful wife, mom, and businesswoman. Underneath her polished exterior, however, she battles low self-esteem and self-doubt. She'd like to experience freedom from the daily barrage of internal criticism. Her efforts at prayer and positive self-talk have not been as helpful as she would like, so she makes an appointment with an IFS therapist. Their meeting might go something like this:

THERAPIST: So glad you are here, Anna. What would you like to work on today?

ANNA: I'm glad to be here too. I'd like to work with the critical part of me. I just can't get away from it. I feel like nothing I ever do is good enough and that I'll just never feel like I measure up.

[1. Find]

THERAPIST: I'd love to help you with that. Let's start by seeing if we can find that part of you. When you notice this internal criticism, where do you feel it in your body? How do you experience this critical part?

ANNA: In my forehead. I notice my forehead scrunches up and also my shoulders—they get tense.

[2. Focus]

THERAPIST: So you notice it in your forehead and your shoulders. Can you focus on those for a moment? Notice that scrunching in your forehead and tension in your shoulders and just let your attention be with that part as you experience it.

ANNA: Okay.

[3. Flesh Out]

THERAPIST: What else do you notice about it?

ANNA: I dunno. This is kind of weird, but I just got this image of an angry old man with a megaphone.

THERAPIST: Great. So thank this part for showing itself to you. See if it's aware of you there with it.

ANNA: Yeah. He seems to notice me. He kind of dropped the megaphone down a little and turned his head toward me.

[4. Feel]

THERAPIST: How do you feel toward this angry old man?

ANNA: I don't like him. I want him to go away and quit yelling at me.

THERAPIST: So there's a concerned part of you that doesn't like him and would like his yelling to stop?

ANNA: Yeah, I guess so.

THERAPIST: That makes sense. Let the concerned part know that you might be able to help him not have to yell if you can get to know him. See if that concerned part would be willing to step back so you can get to know the angry man.

ANNA: Um, okay. . . . Yeah, it's willing to step back and let me be with him.

[5. BeFriend]

THERAPIST: Good. Now what are you noticing about the man? Is he aware of you?

ANNA: He's looking at me kind of quizzically. Like he's never seen me before. He looks really tired, but he seems to be relaxing a bit now that he knows I'm here.

THERAPIST: Great. Now check and see how you are feeling toward the angry man.

ANNA: Well, I guess I'm kind of curious why he is yelling at me so much.

THERAPIST: Mmm. Let him know you are curious about his yelling and see if he'd like to tell you why he's doing that.

ANNA: Okay. . . . I don't know. This is weird, but I get the impression he is trying to protect me.

[6. Fear]

THERAPIST: Ask him what he's protecting you from, what he's afraid would happen if he didn't yell at you all the time.

ANNA: I just had a memory flash up of my third-grade teacher who yelled at me in front of the whole class when I didn't know the right answer. I was so humiliated. I get the sense that he's trying to help me not be humiliated again. It seems like maybe he yells at me all the time so I'll do everything right and get all the answers right.

THERAPIST: Does that make sense to you why he'd do that? Yes? Let him know that you appreciate him trying to protect you from humiliation.

ANNA: Okay. I just got an image of me as a little girl curled up crying. Like after my teacher yelled at me.

THERAPIST: So the man is trying to protect that little girl, is that right? Can you thank him? How's he doing with that appreciation?

ANNA: Yeah. He just put down the megaphone and sat on the floor. He seems really tired. And grateful that I'm noticing him and appreciating his hard work.

THERAPIST: See how he feels about the job he is doing for you. Is there anything else he'd rather be doing?

ANNA: I get the impression that he hates it. He doesn't like to yell all the time. But he really doesn't want me to be humiliated again. I get the clear sense that he'd rather be a cheerleader. He'd rather be encouraging me.

THERAPIST: Great. Let him know that you see that. That you understand how tired he is and how much he hates the yelling. Ask him if there was another way to prevent you from being humiliated, would he be interested in that?

ANNA: He's definitely interested.

THERAPIST: Let him know that if he would be willing to let you go to that little girl and witness her pain and heal her, that he wouldn't have to yell anymore to protect her and he could be freed up to be a cheerleader or anything else he'd like to do. Would he like that?

ANNA: Oh yeah, definitely. But he doesn't believe that's possible.

THERAPIST: I get that. See if he'd be open to giving you permission to get to know that little girl and watching how it goes, knowing that he can jump back in at any point if he's not feeling okay about it. Is he open to that?

ANNA: Mmm. He's actually kind of excited about it.

This is the way we meet our parts, get to know their positive intent, and help them unblend from us. This therapist is using a Six Fs approach to help her client relate more effectively with her Critic.

And now that you've seen unblending at work, you can apply the same approach to yourself.

Going Deeper:
Getting to know a manager using the Six Fs

Take a moment to settle into a quiet, peaceful space. Take several deep, slow breaths and allow your attention to gradually settle into your body. Close your eyes or let your gaze settle softly on the floor if that's comfortable. Notice what you are experiencing. Pay attention to any emotions, thoughts, and physical sensations.

Think of a manager that you'd like to get to know.

Now you can use the Six Fs exercise to get to know this amazing part of you. Pause to reflect on each step, allowing it the time it needs to become clear for you.

1. **Find** *the part:*

What are you feeling?

Where do you feel it in your body?

What physical sensations do you notice when this part is present?

2. **Focus** *on the part:*

Direct your attention toward how you experience that part in your body. Focus on it.

What do you notice about it?

3. Flesh *it out:*

What else do you notice about the part?

How do you experience it?

Is there an image that represents this part?

Can you notice anything else about the way you perceive this part?

4. Feel *toward it:*

How do you feel *toward* the part? (This is a Spiritual MRI. If I feel anything toward the part other than the Eight Cs, I have another part blended with my God Image. I need to invite that part to unblend so I can relate to my first part from my God Image. The goal is to relate to all my parts from my God Image.)

5. BeFriend *the part:*

Let it know you appreciate its positive intent and how it's trying to help you. See if it will receive your appreciation and respond positively. See how the part is doing with your God Image present.

Ask that part of you if it would like to show you anything about itself.

- Where did it learn to help you in this way?

- What parts of you is it protecting?

- What is its role in your internal system?

- How does it feels about its role?

- Is there anything else it would rather be doing?

6. What is its **Fear?**

Ask the part what it is afraid would happen if it didn't show up and help you in this way. What outcome is it trying to prevent?[44]

Spend as much time as you'd like getting to know this part of you. When it feels complete, gently bring your awareness away from your internal experience and back into the room around you. It may help to focus on deepening your breath, noticing the ground beneath your feet, or listening for any sounds that you can hear.

What was that exercise like for you?

What did you learn?

Did anything surprise you?

Has your experience shifted in any way?

Because parts often show themselves in a visual way, it can be helpful to draw out a quick sketch of your manager here:

Journal anything you want to remember here:

Now that you've had the opportunity to get to know one or more of your own *proactive* managers, we can move on to discovering our *reactive* firefighters. We'll talk about these in the next chapter.

Discussion Questions

- Have you ever struggled with the harsh narrative of an Internal Critic? How have you tried to deal with it in the past? What has the result been? What is it like to consider that Critic is trying to actually help you?

- Do you recall a time in which you connected with someone in a deeply God Image kind of way? That is to say, in authentic spirituality? Have you ever felt the experience of hearing from someone else's Spiritualizer? What were those two experiences like for you?

- What aspects of the conversation with Anna about her Critic/Judge manager resonate the most with you?

- How does the idea that there are no bad parts, only bad roles compare to what you've previously believed?

- What part did you get to know in the Six Fs exercise? Did you learn anything about this part that surprised you? How is it trying to help you?

MEETING OUR FIREFIGHTERS

Parts that work hard to *stop* pain

This parts talk is all well and good for people whose parts are doing socially acceptable things like serving and pleasing. But when our parts are doing things we're horribly ashamed of and can't stop doing, the tone of the conversation shifts. We squirm a bit more and look around to make sure no one's listening.

In this chapter we take a kind and clear-eyed look at the hard-working reactive protectors called firefighters. Several might look familiar to you. In IFS, we describe a firefighter as a protector part that goes into action in order to numb an exile's pain or distract the system from it. But by now, you know a shorter version. A firefighter is trying to rescue you from a flare-up of pain.

Firefighter: A burdened protector part that attempts to extinguish the pain of exile(s) reactively, after the exile has been triggered. Common firefighter strategies include addictions, disordered eating, self-harm, violence, dissociation, obsession, compulsion, fantasy, rage.

Let's just put it out there—tangling with our firefighters can be difficult, scary work. We can feel like we're wrestling with monsters in the dark, and sometimes we're sure *the monster is us*.

But stay with me. You're in for a few surprises and a whole lot of relief.

Firefighters are not our most popular parts. They are the rogues in our gallery, our own personal Masters of Excess. They *mean* well, really. But they tend to rush in and make a huge mess of things, in the process scaring the socks off all the people around them. Sometimes even the people whose parts they are.

That's because firefighter parts usually cope by using behaviors that are neither safe nor socially acceptable: drinking too much, acting out sexually, cutting, dissociating, raging, contemplating suicide or homicide. Each of these "solutions" is meant to help but ends up creating misery in our lives and the lives of those around us.

That's a shame because firefighters are actually wonderful parts of us. And yes, you heard me correctly.

Just like real firefighters, they see a "fire" (of painful emotion) and break down the doors and spray water all over the priceless oil painting in the living room because they are single-minded in their goal: to stop the fire. They don't have the luxury of noticing or caring about that priceless piece of art because . . . *fire!*

They are wonderful, those alcoholic, sexually addicted, suicidal parts—I believe that with all my heart. I can work with firefighters all day long and see beauty in literally everyone, no matter what hot mess their burdened firefighters are busy making. I know perfectly well they have no intention of hurting that painting, or their wives, or their kids. And because firefighters really are just trying to help, I can help them find better ways to put out the fire. Which comes as a great relief to them—and to everyone else.

So let's talk about these scary, messy, unruly parts of us to see if we can understand what in the world they are up to.

HEROES IN SMOKE-FILLED ROOMS

People who are dominated by firefighters often cluster in "firefighter-friendly" areas: bars, nightclubs, Las Vegas, strip clubs, parties. But firefighters can operate by stealth as well. They may exist quietly within manager-dominated communities—like churches, businesses, and honor societies—while only occasionally or secretly taking over. In those environments, firefighters tend to feel even more shame and hide deeper and deeper underground.

Remember, firefighters are just good parts stuck in bad roles. They are doing the same thing as managers: trying to fix the pain the exiles are carrying. When that pain gets out in front—let's say when we are turned down for a date, or get in a big fight with a partner, or make a mistake on an important project—the firefighters jump in to try to make the pain go away. And let's be honest, raging, drinking, sexting, and other firefighter favorites *do* help to distract from the pain. For a while. And then those solutions make the mess bigger.

To make the situation worse, firefighters are hated by pretty much everyone. They are hated by manager parts, other firefighters, and most of the people outside of us: the church, spouses, teachers, law enforcement, and sometimes even therapists. Firefighters are at war with, it seems, the whole darn world.

In chapter 1 we noted how the apostle James seemed to understand the nature of parts when he wrote: "What causes fights and quarrels among you? Don't they come from your desires that battle within you?"[45] Oh, yes. That's exactly it. Our parts are at war.

Take our manager parts, who often seriously hate our firefighters. Our managers are the ones who, the morning after the firefighter has been in control, say "How could I have done that again? What is wrong with me?" Managers would like to see the firefighters locked in the basement forever, or better yet, thrown out of the system entirely. The problem is, if we did that, we would lose the wonderful qualities the firefighters could bring to our system (more on those in a minute)—qualities that we don't have access to when they are carrying the burdens of extreme behavior.

Rather than trying to throw parts out of the system—which, by the way, doesn't work because it is impossible to get rid of any of our parts—we can move toward them with love and compassion and gratitude for how hard they are trying to help. We can also move toward them with a curiosity to hear their story.

This conversation gets so loaded with suffering, guilt, and shame for all concerned that I'm going to take you back to my cookie story for insight.

Let's say I have a firefighter who powerfully believes that Oreos are the answer to life. At least in certain vulnerable moments. And again, I'm only speaking hypothetically of course. (Not that I would actually have a part like this.) When I'm feeling uncomfortable, rejected, anxious, or not good enough, that firefighter part shows up with a bag of Oreos to try to comfort me in my pain.

Eat this now. You'll feel better.

And it works—to the firefighter's credit—for a minute, anyway, because I feel a little better from the sugar rush and pleasure of eating. Of course, three minutes later, a manager part that's upset about all the calories I just ate shows up and yells at the Oreo-eating firefighter.

You ate . . . WHAT? You weren't EVER going to do that again. You dumb, fat slob!

It all starts to feel pretty yucky as my parts, as James so wisely described, go to war with each other.

But what if there's another way?

What if, instead of aligning with my manager and shaming the Oreo eater and letting my internal critical tell me I'm a fat slob, I invited those parts that are angry at the Oreo eater to unblend or step back for a minute? What if, instead of getting mad, I became curious? *Moved toward* the difficult parts?

Specifically, what if I simply asked the Oreo eater what it is afraid would happen if it didn't make me eat Oreos when I'm hurting? I can use my Six Fs, introduced in the previous chapter, to bring curiosity and compassion to my internal battles.

I might find out my Oreo-eating firefighter developed when I experienced painful situations as a child and the only comfort around was food. Maybe I felt like I had nowhere else to turn for help with my problems, but eating made me feel better. For a moment.

With that awareness, I might actually experience compassion and appreciation for this eating firefighter part. After all, it's been pretty resourceful when there wasn't other comfort available and tried to help minimize the pain of my circumstances.

With this new posture of compassion and curiosity, I can now turn toward the part that's angry at the Eater. I may discover that my angry manager part developed to protect me when my childhood school circumstances taught me I would only be loved or have friends if I were perfect. It is trying, in its criticism, to help me avoid "not-perfect" (because of eating too much). It's trying to help me to be loved.

Wow. Suddenly my disgust at the internal war is transformed into gratitude. In the process, I find my calm, clear-minded God Image. I also gain the ability to make a different choice than eating Oreos or being furious with myself when I'm in pain. I now have options.

When I hold compassion for my parts, I have hope of giving them access to my God Image, which is the key to healing their pain. Once they are healed, they can transform and are freed up to stop eating or being angry and start doing something much more helpful.

When I hold compassion for my parts, I have hope of giving them access to my God Image, which is the key to healing their pain.

You'll find hands-on help and how to do this with your unique firefighters in the next chapter. For now, let's get to know a few of these hard-working, underappreciated firefighters and some of the strategies on which they typically rely. The same principle goes here as it did for managers: firefighters are much more complex than just the strategies they are using. But identifying some of their more familiar behaviors can help us to respond more helpfully.

I'll begin with one I know well.

GET SMALL

This firefighter is mine, definitely mine. And it's honestly kind of funny trying to get small when you are a five-foot, nine-inch woman. But my firefighter has learned to get small in more ways than one.

Remember my exiles from high school? Rejected, ashamed, stupid, less-than, not included? Yep. Old, familiar parts of me that still occasionally get activated in my adult life. And when they do, I start shutting down. My eyes drop to the floor. Arms and legs cross. I notice myself moving closer to walls, looking for doors, and thinking up strategies for exiting the environment. I pretend to be engrossed in my phone, do my best not to speak, or if I have to, I immediately ask someone else a question that redirects the conversation away from me.

You might be familiar with the three common responses to danger: fight, flight, or freeze. Well, Get Small is kind of a cross between flight and freeze. The body freezes when it can't escape, and the person inside "flees" by becoming as invisible as possible. For people surrounded by big personalities or big situations where "fight" or "get big" seems impossible, Get Small is a pretty resourceful response. Unfortunately, this strategy usually takes away a person's voice and ability to speak into a situation or use appropriate power to take self-protective action.

DISSOCIATION

Dissociation is a superresourceful firefighter strategy that works on a continuum, from mostly healthy to not so much. Many of us dissociate every day in mild ways: we daydream, stare out the window, get lost in fantasy thoughts, or otherwise briefly check out.

Dissociation is likely to be stuck in a firefighter role, however, when it consistently takes over when painful situations (or things that remind us of painful situations) are present. At these times, our bodies are present but . . .

We blankly stare into space and become unaware of what is happening around us.

We lose time.

We disappear into Facebook and realize three hours have passed.

We start driving and have no idea how we got where we ended up.

We binge watch Netflix for hours at a time.

Dissociation takes us out of our lives for the moment so that our exiles don't have to feel whatever it is they are afraid of feeling. It takes us out of our bodies in certain ways. If what's happening around us is scary or painful or unsafe in some way, this part actually transports us somewhere else, even though our bodies can't leave the situation. An amazing way that our parts learn to cope, when you think about it.

Of course, when we are dissociated, we can't take action to protect ourselves, so it winds up leaving us more vulnerable rather than less. But it is a strong and faithful rescuer intent on getting us away from hard things.

RAGING/AGGRESSION

Especially if your life has been touched by someone who rages or is aggressive or verbally or physically violent, I want you to know that your pain matters. Understanding what rage is trying to do doesn't make its behavior okay. And your exiles are probably pretty darned scared of it.

Rage as a firefighter strategy often works overtime to protect small, scared exile parts that feel powerless or disrespected. When the pain of those exiles is activated by present circumstances, rage jumps in to create the illusion of power and influence. It often tries to scare away the person or situation that feels threatening so the exiles it protects will feel safe. It's the *fight* response of fight, flight, or freeze.

Like all firefighters, Rage is trying to help the exiles, even though it is doing so in a way that ultimately makes them feel more out of control and less respected and heard. By driving people away who might comfort those exiles, it is unwittingly creating the situation it fears most.

Rage has lots of faces. The most obvious is physical: throwing things, hitting people, threatening others, screaming. Rage tries to help us get "big" when we perceive a threat to our well-being so the perceived threat will back off and leave us alone. It is an effort to create empowerment in the face of powerlessness. Unfortunately, it ultimately makes us lose control and frightens the snot out of those around us.

Sadly, parents who cope with Rage firefighter strategies sometimes create the very same firefighters in their terrified children.

Then there's Rage that comes out sideways, including sarcasm, biting humor, edgy remarks. You know this firefighter. It's the one others struggle to seat at the wedding because it's likely to say something that will offend. This version of rage lets everyone around know they'd better be on guard, because at any moment they could get hit by verbal shrapnel.

Rage is highly successful at sabotaging intimacy. Intimacy, after all, triggers the vulnerability that "if you really knew me, you wouldn't love me," and sideways rage figures it's "better to hurt you first so you can't hurt me."

That's rough. And sad. My heart hurts for this panicked firefighter trying to look so tough.

It is important, however, to notice the difference between a burdened Rage firefighter and a healthy expression of strong anger. One is trying to move people away; the other is trying to communicate authentically in order to move toward real relationship. That distinction can feel confusing, I know. We don't tend to have a lot of models for handling anger well.

> A Rage firefighter is trying to move people away. Healthy anger is trying to move toward real relationship.

Here's the difference: a healthy God Image, speaking on behalf of a part that has experienced some injury or harm, might say in a calm and respectful tone, "Dave, I need to let you know that I feel very angry about the comment you made about me in front of the office staff today. I was deeply hurt when you shared a mistake I made for what seemed to be the purpose of humiliating me. Would you be willing to help me understand why you said that, or offer an apology in front of those people?"

Notice I can still feel strong anger in my authentic self and can listen to it telling me that I've had a boundary crossed, which will motivate me to say how I feel and ask for what I need.

That's God Image at work—very different from the burdened, raging firefighter that sounds more like, "**!!!###**!!!!"

One moves toward. The other moves against. There's a world of difference.

EATING

Here we go. This is one of my favorite firefighters because this part eats Oreos. Lots of them. Or doesn't eat anything at all. Or eats and purges. All are differing ways to use food to feel better, and that seems kind of sweet in its own weird way because, like, all the grandmas in the world conspire to make this a thing.

"Have you eaten today?"

"Would you like more mashed potatoes?"

"We need to put meat on your bones."

Eating is a lot like spending and sex in that it is a necessary part of living. When we eat simply to meet our nutritional needs and enjoy the tastes and textures of various foods, we probably are in an unburdened place with this part: a good part in a good role.

If, however, we are eating, restricting, dieting, or binging in order to feel better about ourselves, to numb pain, to mitigate low self-image, or to wrestle control from someone else in our lives, then eating has likely become a firefighter strategy.

And oh, man, in a culture where literally everything seems to ride on how you look, this firefighter has lots of opportunity to develop.

Eating firefighters are profoundly complex and can play various functions and roles, depending on the pain they are protecting. The exiles typically behind Eating firefighters hold beliefs like "not good enough," "ugly," "worthless," "out of control," "unchosen," and "powerless."

This firefighter might attempt to provide comfort through a sugar rush or high, it could be masking the pain of low self-worth ("If I look a certain way, I will be valuable"), or it might attempt to restore control through restricting something no one else has power over. It is clever and adept at resisting change when it feels misunderstood.

Eating firefighters are some of the deadliest we face in the mental health world. I have serious respect for their power. They seem sweet or helpful until they are not—and they are often so totally not. But they are working hard to solve a problem and are stubborn in their persistence. They deserve our care and compassion. And our God Image healing. When they are present in extreme forms, they need the support and care of a team of eating disorder specialists, nutritionists, and health consultants.

DRINKING

Not all alcohol use is the strategy of a burdened firefighter. You can have wine with the girls or beer at the game and not be locked in the throes of this damaging firefighter.

With deep compassion, I also need to say that when we must have a drink to deal with stress or anxiety, when drinking starts controlling us, when we can't go out or come home or get up without a drink, when we turn to a drink to help with our pain, we've ventured into firefighter territory. Now it's a part stuck in an unhelpful role, trying hard to make our pain go away but clearly making it worse.

A typical Drinking firefighter develops to comfort a person whose exiles feel not good enough, unchosen, or worthless by—literally—drowning the terrible feelings that accompany those beliefs.

Unfortunately, its presence creates more pain—DUIs, arguments, blackouts, poor choices, spending, accidents, hangovers. And these result in broken relationships and all manner of difficulties, which heap more pain on the exiles it is trying to protect. And that fuels more drinking. On and on the cycle goes.

In our culture, it is easy to get caught up with this firefighter because it is so pervasive. Alcohol is offered at the game, the dinner party, the frat party, the business dinner, the wedding, the graduation, the weekend boating trip, and all over the media in every way conceivable. Ever tried to go to the beach or a Super Bowl party and *not* encounter drinking?

If we can take it or leave it, don't turn to it when we're uncomfortable, and don't miss it when it's not there, then alcohol may not be a firefighter for us. However, if we need a glass or a shot to relax us when we're stressed, to make us happy when we're sad, to chill us out when we're anxious, or to celebrate when we're victorious, we have the hallmarks of firefighter activity: using alcohol to numb us from our reality.

DRUGGING

Much like alcohol, drugs alter our awareness and experience of reality. If reality is painful or difficult, drugs offer a fairly straightforward coping strategy. The drugging firefighter has one mantra: *escape, escape, escape.* Make the pain—whatever its flavor—better for a while.

The supposed solution to the pain is a grand hoax, of course, and once a person is caught in the spell of this firefighter, addiction has often become a bigger problem than the drug. The solution has now become the problem, leaving the exiles behind it in ever-increasing pain.

SEXUAL ACTING OUT

In our culture with virtual, immediate, anonymous access to literally any form of sexual behavior imaginable, sex has become a perfect strategy for a burdened firefighter.

With sexual mores changing faster than we can blink, how do we know if we have a firefighter on our hands? Is it a type of sexual behavior? Or frequency?

Neither, actually. We know it's a firefighter by what it's trying to do, and the effect it has on us.

If our sexual expression stems from intimate connection and leaves us feeling treasured, connected, intimate, and bonded, then it is likely the beautiful expression of what our sexuality was designed by God to be. If our sexual expression (even within marriage) is regularly compensating for our feeling alone or unworthy and leaves us or our partner feeling used, manipulated, pressured, objectified, ashamed, and alone, then our sexuality might have morphed into a firefighter.

If we are using sex in any way to try to feel better, to cope with pain, or to numb our hurts, we've got a firefighter—even if it's occurring within marriage.

Whether through pornography, sexting, affairs, strip clubs, prostitution, or various other behaviors, sexual acting out can also be highly addictive. Sex releases powerful reward chemicals in the brain that immediately create a feel-good response. When stuck in firefighter mode, a sexual part will be trying hard to soothe and protect exiles that feel alone, broken, or not wanted. But it winds up creating a self-fulfilling prophecy as it destroys relationships that could mitigate those exile feelings if allowed to flourish in healthy ways.

Here, we see another hallmark indicator of a firefighter: it feels good in the short run and bad in the long run.

A firefighter feels good in the short run and bad in the long run.

The Sexual Acting Out firefighter shows up in my offices regularly, and trust me, folks, this one feels really, really bad in the long run.

Wounded partners of people with this firefighter commonly ask, "How could you do this [have an affair, compulsively watch pornography, have sex with a prostitute] to me? How could you do this to the kids? Don't you love us?"

It's a valid question, and yet it doesn't understand the nature of a firefighter. The firefighter of Sexual Acting Out is oblivious to the partner, kids, family, reputation, church attendance, or any other facet of the person's life. Sexual Acting Out is after one thing only: making the pain of feeling alone or worthless feel better. Even if just for a moment. Knowing this helps us understand better how to help it to heal. Yet as with all firefighters, the behavior is not okay just because it is driven by an exile's pain.

SPENDING

Here's another tricky one to discern, because spending is a natural and important part of our daily lives. We have to buy all kinds of things to survive, from groceries to clothing to school supplies.

We suspect that spending has become a firefighter, however, when we spend to make ourselves feel better, regardless of the price tag. If I buy a $5 bracelet because it makes me feel pretty or desirable, then it may be a firefighter. If I buy a $150 pair of shoes because they are important for my work environment but not necessary for my self-image, then it's probably not a firefighter.

Shopping is a particularly tricky firefighter strategy in our culture where personal worth is often quantified by affluence—or the appearance of affluence—and spending creates a high that mitigates pain. This firefighter can be masking exiles that believe "I'm not enough" or "I don't have value and worth."

Spending can also be a stealth firefighter because it may not necessarily create additional problems in our lives. If it is within the budget of the spender, then there may not be financial consequences like bankruptcy, debt, and inability to pay bills. However, if the next time you get in a conflict with your beloved you go shopping to feel better, you just might have a firefighter. Even if you can afford that $100 blouse. And maybe especially if you can't.

If I get on Amazon Prime and spend hours surfing through consumer goods because it allows me to check out and stop feeling stressed, rejected, not good enough, or broken, then I'm using the shopping environment as a firefighter. Even if I don't buy anything, or wind up returning everything I bought.

Whoa!

Someone with an advanced Shopping firefighter may buy more than one of essentially the same thing—two of the same pair of shoes, the same blouse in three different colors—or may have boxes and boxes of new purchases at home that have never been opened. Or clothes with tags still attached hanging in the closet. This is because it is the transaction of spending that creates the dopamine high—the feel-good effect the firefighter is going for—not the fulfillment of any actual need for the item being purchased.

You could say that hoarding is a deeply advanced firefighter in this realm, acquiring or holding on to possessions in order to feel secure or safe. That's why a compassionate response to hoarding looks beyond the clutter to address the reason behind the behavior and to comfort the exile that is afraid of not having enough or being unsafe.

As with most protectors, this one can be handed down to the third and fourth generation. I've experienced this in my own family. I hit the jackpot with my husband because he loves to go to the grocery store and to cook, and I do not. But I do love to clean. So about ten years into our marriage we decided to switch food-preparation roles, and he started grocery shopping and cooking, and I started doing the menu planning and cleanup. That arrangement has honestly been the best thing ever.

Except, I can't have you over if he is out of town because we'd have to order pizza or something.

Now, we have never not had enough to eat. Unless you're counting that time when we were first married. I was in a graduate program that had a comma and a lot of zeroes in the price tag, and we pretty much ate only pasta for a couple of years. But we were in our twenties and thought that was great.

Nevertheless, our pantry has always had food in it.

Now, my husband loves a good BOGO sale. He is notorious for buying large quantities of various nonperishable goods and keeping our shelves full of them. In fact, as I speak, we have about ten years' worth of Costco-sized bottles of olive oil in the pantry. Some of it could be in my will when I pass. So, if you are hankering to sauté garlic—c'mon over and we can hook you up. Olive oil, we've got. Same goes for jars of Prego. And boxes of cereal.

One day my husband looked in the pantry and realized the many jars of Prego meant more to him than getting a good deal. They meant *enough*. We would have *enough* if there was a need. Never mind that we've never had a need. But his father had.

My father-in-law survived the Holocaust. His father and older brother were taken to a Nazi camp while he was left to care for his mother and the remaining ten siblings in a tiny Dutch town terrorized by Nazi occupation. They often did not have enough food to eat, and with many mouths to feed, having enough was a real concern. When the family was able, they fled to the United States.

So my husband, looking in the pantry in our always-enough home, realized he carried the worry that there wouldn't be enough from a generation that wasn't his and an experience he hadn't known.

That Prego was about much more than a sale. It was protection from the Nazis. That's a generational firefighter.

CUTTING/SELF-HARM

Okay, friends, these protectors are tough. If your life or the life of someone you love has been impacted by this firefighter, you may feel some fear or avoidance around this section. That makes sense. You have full permission to skip right over it—and any other sections that are triggering—and keep reading elsewhere. Spend some time with the parts of you that carry pain around these topics, giving them compassion and care. These guys are hard, and I'm truly sorry for your pain.

Cutting and Self-Harm are complex firefighters that work in a variety of ways. They are trying to make *emotional* pain better by inflicting *physical* harm or pain. That may not make sense on the surface, but it does once we understand what's going on underneath.

They are another example of how burdened protector strategies actually create the very thing they are most trying to avoid, and that is pain.

Cutting, Burning, or other types of Self-Harm can take over for a variety of reasons. Sometimes they are polarized with a Dissociative part that causes a person not to feel. Self-Harm then steps in to create pain, rationalizing that feeling pain is preferable to feeling completely empty or numb on the inside.

Polarized: When two parts in a system are working in opposition to each other. Managers and firefighters are often polarized. Each part strives to counteract the behavior of the other part.

The Cutting firefighter is, in a sense, reminding the person that they are alive, because at least when they cut, they can feel something. Anything. Which is better than the alternative.

At other times, the Cutting part reflects the self-loathing of an exile that cuts to manage the exile belief that "I am bad." It is an external way to manifest internal pain—a way to punish the person for being so "bad" or "unworthy."

That often creates more shame and humiliation for the person who is cutting. Now that person has to wear long sleeves in ninety-degree weather to hide the scars, which in turn makes relating to others difficult, which reinforces the original pain of the exiles.

SUICIDAL

Although in many ways a Self-Harm firefighter seems similar to a Suicidal one, they are often working toward different ends with different means.

Suicidal firefighters are terrifying parts. Let's just honor that for a minute. This firefighter strategy can focus only on the cry of the exile: "Make the pain stop!" As a result, it has extremely narrow vision; it can see only one way of ending the severe pain of the exiles it is protecting, and that is to stop living.

This firefighter scares everyone around it, including loved ones, parents, pastors, and therapists. But like all other firefighters, it also is a hard-working part trying its best to come up with a solution to pain that has gotten out of control. The exiles it is trying to protect are in tremendous, overwhelming anguish.

Sometimes, the Suicidal firefighter is protecting an exile that feels unnoticed or overlooked. In this role it is trying to gain the attention and care that is craved but perhaps not being received in other ways. Or it is blinded by the suffering of the exiles and just can't see another way to make the pain stop. It's not that it truly wants to die; it just desperately wants to end the pain, and for whatever reason, death seems like the only option.

Either way, this firefighter is formidable, and like any other burdened part, it needs to be taken very seriously. Suicidal parts need the care and support of skilled therapists as well as wise and informed loved ones. Suicidal parts also need to experience different ways to help make the pain better, which is ultimately done best by healing the exiles that drive it.

We always, always want to listen to Suicidal firefighters, believe them, and get them help as quickly as possible. They can be freed up when the pain they are trying to cope with is unburdened, but that usually requires strong professional support and a network of caring loved ones.

HOMICIDAL

Okay, I get chills just thinking about this one. Maybe you do, too. This firefighter strategy is perhaps the most feared of all because the behaviors it considers, or engages in, are so destructive. Entire TV shows are scripted around characters who have homicidal firefighters because the public is so fascinated (and horrified) with how their minds work.

Homicidal firefighters are sometimes working in partnership with raging parts whose anger burden is so extreme that killing someone—for example, in extreme cases of domestic violence—seems like a good way to end a problem. Homicide becomes a part's "solution" to resolving an escalating relational conflict.

In similar circumstances, homicidal firefighters may be a part's way of expressing unbearable inner rage, self-loathing, and despair: sometimes through retribution toward a perceived enemy/tormentor, or as vehicle through which to give voice to the rage of powerlessness into a society that the individual experiences as hurtful. Homicide in these contexts is a burdened strategy to express rage and pain, or to gain perceived control over an environment in which the person feels powerless.

In other contexts, homicidal firefighters may be seeking to enact mercy, as is sometimes the case in parental murder-suicides. The parent's primary firefighter is suicidal (seeking to help end pain by ending the individual's life) but a secondary homicidal firefighter develops that ends the children's lives, to spare them from the pain and abandonment of parental suicide. In this context, the homicidal firefighter is motivated by a burdened sense of compassion.

In the rare instance when sociopathy is present (the God Image is so profoundly obscured that the individual has no access to parts that feel empathy or remorse for inflicting destruction), the homicidal part could be at work seeking power, glory, or fame. In this case, it might be protecting exiles that feel profoundly powerless and insignificant.

Notice that in every circumstance the intent of the firefighter is positive: resolving conflict, having a voice, creating agency, establishing meaning (via fame), creating emotional safety. And yet, as with every burdened protector, the outcome of the behavior makes pain worse. Homicidal firefighters are obviously serious and very dangerous. While the consequences of their actions require stiff protective measures and firm legal boundaries, this is still a burdened part like any other, and behind it lie wounded exiles desperately needing healing and unburdening. Again, this requires the close intervention of a network of professionals and very clear and serious boundaries. Yet how comforting to know that even this firefighter makes sense. Homicidal parts profoundly obstruct the God Image within, but they do not destroy it. Their strategy may be terrifying, but their desire, like all protectors, is to help. Help with pain. And like all other protectors, they sadly only intensify it.

COMPASSION FOR OUR "MONSTERS"

We opened this chapter comparing our industrious firefighters to monsters we wrestle in the dark. Our firefighters do often repel us and others, and leave hurt and destruction, guilt and shame in their wake. Over time, however, and after repeated failures to tame them, we commonly come to believe that "monstrous" is just who we are.

But now you know that's not true.

Your firefighters are well-intended parts stuck in bad roles. They can be helped much more effectively when we consider the goals that our firefighters are trying to achieve, and show consideration for how long and how hard they've been trying unsuccessfully to help. While needing firm boundaries, our firefighter parts often wish they could be freed to do the very opposite of what they are doing. They just don't know how.

In the next chapter we will look at practical steps we can take toward personal change.

Discussion Questions

- Which of the firefighters listed in this chapter can you most identify with?

- Which are most upsetting to you?

- How does learning that firefighters have good intentions affect your attitude toward the way they act out in your life?

- What is it like for you to consider that firefighters are trying to help us with pain, but that doesn't make their behavior okay? How do you make sense of that?

- Why do firefighters tend to win out over managers?

8

FIREFIGHTERS GONE WILD

Three solutions for firefighter chaos

Y ou've noticed a common and heartbreaking theme with our fire-fighters: They are trying to manage pain in the best way they know how, yet they often don't see the damaging, frightening, and dangerous consequences of their actions. Driving their behavior is the pain of the exiles, which they will go to any lengths to extinguish.

So, what does this mean for us practically? Are we supposed to feel sorry for these parts and allow them to drink and drug and rage and kill people? Are we saying that because they mean well, we should "turn the other cheek" and ignore the pain and devastation they inflict?

No, friends, not at all. As with managers in the previous section, to know and embrace your troublesome parts is not the same thing as saying anything goes.

Becoming aware of firefighters' intent allows us to make sense of their behavior, which allows us to respond to them more effectively. Not to condone or excuse their actions, but to be wise in our responses and to actually give them the greatest possibility of change.

CASE STUDIES IN FIRE PREVENTION

If we boil it down, there are three situations in which we typically encounter firefighters, each of which invites a different response. We can describe the situations as:

1. Limited relationship
2. Significant relationship
3. Oh dear, those little buggers are mine

Situation Number One: Limited Relationship

When I am in limited relationship with someone whose firefighter doesn't significantly impact me—let's say, the raging driver on the freeway who cuts me off, or the aggressive lady in the ten-items-or-less line who has five hundred items. What to do?

Big picture: It is helpful to simply hold respectful awareness of what might be going on in that person and what's coming up in me. I stay in God Image and avoid my own protector meltdown, and that allows me to respond with calm wisdom when others are out of control. It also invites me deeper into my own healing.

But let's look at things in more detail.

Let's say the lady pulls into the checkout line and starts, with angry entitlement, unloading her entire cart of groceries when the sign clearly says ten items or fewer. I'm sure you are much more compassionate than me, but typically in that situation my Irritable/Judging/Controlling parts show up and start telling me terrible things about this lady and her evil heart. My Irritable part might start clearing my throat and exchanging frustrated glances with the other ten-item customers and looking intently at the ten-item sign when she glances in my direction. My judging part is certain she is the worst human on the planet and lives her wicked life oblivious to the needs of others.

I know—it's ugly.

If my Controlling part is strong enough—mine is too polarized with my Pleaser part to do this—I might even tell her she's doing it wrong in a frustrated tone of voice. All the while, I'm becoming more angry, more irritable, more impatient, and more self-righteous and condemning. By the time I get to the cashier, I'm about to explode because my protector parts have taken over in the way they best know how to deal with my inconvenience. I've lost complete access to my God Image, and I might lose a good bit of time after this encounter in the Vortex of Nasty.

We've probably all been there.

Now, take the same situation, except this time I have an awareness of parts. The lady angrily pulls into the checkout line with her five hundred items, and my Irritable/Judging/Controlling parts start to get activated. I notice that I'm feeling things that aren't the Eight Cs, so I know I have parts present. I gently turn my attention inward, find out which parts have jumped in, and ask them if they'd be willing to unblend or step back just a little—so they are not overwhelming me—in order for me to stay in my God Image and hear what's going on for them.

When they do step back, I spontaneously regain my calm, curious, clear-thinking perspective and can sit with them and hear their fears.

Perhaps my Irritable part is worried that I'll be late to my meeting and is trying to protect me from the pain of appearing irresponsible. Maybe my Controlling part is trying to create safety for me—by pushing others around to meet my agenda—because in my life, I've often felt my needs are not as important as others' needs. Or, I could learn that my Judging part is trying to help me feel better about myself because I've done things in the past that disobey rules, and that part wants me to feel better about myself because "at least I'm not as bad as this lady."

Notice how in this place I can remain calm and compassionate for all the worry and annoyance that is being accessed within me, yet I'm still able to be clear minded enough to make decisions that actually will help.

Now I have options. I could choose another line, leave my groceries and come back to shop later, stay put and remind myself that I have plenty of time to make the meeting, or whatever else might be helpful. At least I'm not being flooded with all those destabilizing thoughts and emotions that make me irrational, impulsive, and even hurtful.

When my parts take over, I tend to offend from the victim position—feeling justified in doing or saying hurtful things because I feel like a victim—which winds up hurting others *and* me.

When I hear from my parts but am not overtaken by them, I can make healthy choices to take care of myself while maintaining my best self and my self-control and integrity.

In this place of parts awareness, people whose parts activate me actually become a difficult gift in my life. As Schwartz would say, they become my "tor-mentors." They bring up the parts of me that most need healing, so in this way they mentor me in my personal and spiritual growth.

Tor-mentor: An IFS term for an activating situation or person. By noticing what parts become active in oneself in response to a tor-mentor, an individual will be able to identify their own burdened parts that need healing. Thus, "tormenting" people and situations are a great gift to one's own personal growth and healing.

In this case, by turning my attention to what is coming up in me, I learn that my exile that hasn't had its needs honored needs deeper healing. Now I can attend to this part of me with compassion and without getting sidetracked by pointless anger at a stranger.

This perspective also allows me to honor what could be going on inside others. I can recognize that the angry and entitled part of this lady who pulled into the ten-item line is not who she truly is—her God Image—but simply a part of her that has taken over in this moment. Perhaps she is a single mom with a sick child at home and desperately needs to get checked out quickly, and this was the shortest line. Perhaps English is not her first language and she didn't see or couldn't read the ten-item sign. Perhaps she has a history of abuse and a Pushy part of her has developed in a way to try to get her needs met.

I have no idea what it might be, but in my God Image I have many compassionate options to consider. I might even be able to extend a kindness to her in some small way.

Jesus lived out this parts compassion in spades. John 8 tells one of many of such stories from his life. One day, Jesus was hanging out in the temple when a bunch of religious guys who had set up a woman to be caught in infidelity dragged her out in front of him to be stoned. Their Spiritualizer managers were so activated by her Sexual firefighter that they wanted her dead.

Pause a moment and imagine how wickedly gruesome it would be to literally stone someone to death. We tend to skim over this text because it's familiar, but what was about to happen is nothing short of horrific. For me, the story serves as a sobering reminder that the parts of us that we think are the most righteous and spiritual can sometimes be engaged in the most distorted and wicked behaviors.

These Pharisees were driven to kill in order to appease their Spiritualizer parts. The surprise for them was that Jesus didn't have burdened parts to get activated. He stayed in his God Image (calm, compassionate, clear minded, courageous) and gently, kindly moved toward her with a healing tenderness that met her at exactly the place of her need.

Now, notice how Jesus invited the murderous men to allow her to be a tor-mentor for their activated parts. He calmly invited, "Let any one of you who is without sin be the first to throw a stone at her."[46]

Translation: "Gentlemen, gentlemen. Look at the parts of you that are so activated by this woman, and you will see what *in you* needs healing."

When we stay in God Image, the healing overflows to us and to others, even in casual, seemingly insignificant encounters.

Going Deeper: Getting to know a firefighter from a limited relationship

Think of a recent situation in which you encountered a firefighter in a limited relationship. Where were you and what was happening?

By what firefighter do you think this person was overtaken?

It doesn't make their behavior okay in any way, but can you imagine an exile in them that might make this firefighter's behavior make sense?

What parts got activated in you when this firefighter showed up in them?

List any exiles you're aware of.

List any managers you're aware of.

List any firefighters you're aware of.

Did you respond *from* any of these parts—in other words, allowing them to overtake you and acting as if you were that part? How did it go? What was the outcome?

Now imagine welcoming any parts of yourself that you are aware got activated, honoring their feelings and motivations while speaking or acting from your God Image core. What is that like?

How might your response have differed in this situation if you had approached it in this way?

What would the outcome most likely have been then?

Journal any thoughts, feelings, or observations you might have from this exercise.

Situation Number Two: Significant Relationship

We all realize it's different when we are in significant relationship with someone who has an upfront firefighter. We can walk away from the lady in the ten-item line, but if we are going home every day to a firefighter, what then?

It's especially confusing because this is an area where we often get mixed up in our faith teachings. Commonly applied scriptures like "turn the other cheek"[47] and "forgive seventy times seven"[48] sometimes keep us unwisely victimized by firefighters who consistently bring harm.

Loving and offering authentic forgiveness—which involves knowing what is being forgiven and fully grieving the losses—is not the same as staying in relationship with someone who is dangerous or unrepentant, or saying that what happened didn't matter. Forgiveness and reconciliation are not the same thing. Forgiveness doesn't mean we continue to let others abuse or betray us.

When we are in significant relationship with someone whose firefighter impacts us in deep ways—for example, if a spouse is an abusive alcoholic, or a boss is chronically raging—parts awareness allows us the perspective needed to respond out of our God Image. We can grieve, perceive wisely, and set and follow through with healthy boundaries.

The same is true with a firefighter that presents clear and immediate danger, even if it belongs to a casual acquaintance or only shows up in a familiar relationship on occasion. These firefighters require a more boundaried response.

Consider the firefighter strategy of sexual acting out. How does having a parts awareness help there?

Let's say that Jane has recently discovered that her husband John has been addicted to porn since middle school. His Sexual firefighter developed to comfort the exile part of him that felt not chosen or not desired by his family and the girls in seventh grade. Over the years, that protector behavior has escalated to massage parlors, strip clubs on business trips, and recently, to an affair with a woman at the office. In fact, the behavior has now become a full-blown addiction over which he feels tremendous shame but very little control.

Jane had no idea this betrayal was happening. Now she feels slammed by shock, pain, and shame. How in the world can parts awareness help?

When a parts awareness is *not* present, Jane can fall into a vortex of shame and self-loathing (exiles). She might tell herself she is not beautiful enough, sexual enough, or a good enough spouse (Internal Critic, Self-Blame). She might engage in various exhausting self-improvement strategies such as weight loss, lingerie purchases, and increased sexuality to win his attention back, or she might magnify her pain by playing detective by hunting through cell phone records and credit card bills, or by calling the affair partner (Controlling).

She might take an opposite direction and lash out at him in rage, throw things, immediately divorce him, or tell the kids all manner of horrible things about their no-good, lily-livered, son-of-a-slithery-snake father (Rage, Avoid, Offend from the Victim Position).

A third option is to lunge headfirst into denial. She can ignore the evidence she has of the porn use and affair. She might believe his words, "It only happened once," or "I feel so bad and I'll never do it again." Or she could stay so busy that she can't feel the pain and doesn't have to cope with the losses (Denial, Busyness, Shutdown).

All are understandable ways that Jane's parts are trying to cope with unimaginable pain and loss. They mean well. They just aren't helpful. And they don't see the situation clearly or help her make wise choices. Her parts have taken over and are running the show, but they are unintentionally making her pain worse.

If Jane has parts awareness, she most certainly will feel her pain, and it will be significant. She will realize that the pain of her existing exiles is probably also activated by John's betrayal. Yet by gently asking her various parts (described above) to unblend or step back when they want to take over, she will be able to stay connected to her God Image and will be more able to respond in healthy, healing ways. Sure, the hurt and confusion are still real. But to her own great surprise, she will be able to move toward her pain with healing compassion, see the situation clearly, and make wise choices. She will recognize that his actions are about his pain, not her. These responses spare her time and energy lost in ineffective coping, and free her to grieve her losses in healthy ways.

Jane might hold compassion for the Denial or Depression parts that try to protect her from the full impact of the pain by keeping her busy, shopping, or too depressed to get out of bed. But she can also invite those firefighter parts to unblend so that she can appreciate their efforts without having to be driven by their unhelpful strategies.

By holding parts awareness, Jane has allowed John's painful behavior to become a tor-mentor for her as well. It has activated the parts of her that most need healing. Her pain and trauma from the betrayal of course need primary healing. But she also may discover that throughout her life when she is in pain, a particular protector (perhaps Denial, Shopping, Control, or Rage) often takes over to try to help because she has exiles from an earlier time of life. This could be an invitation to deeper healing in addition to the healing of the betrayal.

A parts awareness can help her see that while John's actions have been traumatic and inexcusable—and are not her fault in any way—they are not *him*. They do not reflect all of who he is. They are simply a part of him.

He could very well love her dearly. The betrayal doesn't necessarily mean the entire marriage was a lie. It certainly might have been, but parts awareness even in something this traumatic allows some of the pain to abate in realizing there is more to John and more to the marriage than his Sexually Acting Out firefighter. If he does his healing work and brings healing to this firefighter, there may even be the option of having something there to rebuild, if she chooses.

When Jane is in her God Image, she can honor all her parts and their feelings while remaining clear minded and courageous. From this standpoint, she can make wise choices—perhaps to start counseling, ask for an in-home therapeutic separation while she observes whether he embraces healing over time, open an independent bank account, or initiate a legal separation. All of these, when coming from her God Image, establish healthy boundaries that care well for her.

In a parts state, Jane might use the word *boundary* to mean "manipulate John to do what I want him to do." (That is a threat, not a boundary.) But in her God Image, she clearly recognizes her only need is to acknowledge her losses, grieve them, and set healthy boundaries that create emotional, spiritual, and physical safety for herself and her children.

I hope you are noticing how parts awareness allows us to be fully present to our real experience. How it invites us to have a healthy relationship with our pain. How it saves us time that our protector parts want to waste doing things that are not truly helpful. How empowering it is.

It is only from our God Image that we can wisely observe the truth of our relationship with someone else's significant firefighter and set healthy, clear boundaries that keep us safe.

Difficult, yes. Necessary, yes. Healthy, absolutely.

That kind of parts awareness is barely imaginable if we've been living with our parts in charge. But it is possible.

Going Deeper: Getting to know a firefighter from a significant relationship

Let's take a moment to explore what this would look like if you do interact with a firefighter in your regular life. This can be difficult territory for any of us to explore. Please treat yourself gently. If anything experiential feels too uncomfortable for the level of support you currently have, stop and tenderly take care of these vulnerable parts of yourself, and seek out someone with IFS training who can guide you in this journey inward. (The appendix, "IFS Resources," includes an IFS therapist locator to assist you with this.)

First, identify and name the firefighter that takes over someone you are close to.

The behavior of a firefighter is *never* excused by the pain it is trying to put out, but do you have a sense of the exile this firefighter may be trying to protect in this person's life? Journal about that.

Now identify the parts (exile, manager, firefighter) of you that come up when this firefighter is present.

List your exiles.

Do you have a sense of where these exiles originated in your life experience? Was it prior to this relationship? Journal your thoughts.

List your managers.

Do you have a sense of which of your exiles these managers are trying to protect? How does it typically work in the short run? In the long run? Journal your answers.

List your firefighters.

Do you have an idea of which of your exiles these firefighters are trying to protect? How does it typically work out in the short run? In the long run? Journal your answers.

Now welcome any parts in you that you've identified. Honor what they are feeling or how they are trying to help you. See if they would step back and let you connect with your calm, clear-minded, courageous God Image within. Journal what you notice.

Notice how much clarity, courage, compassion, and strength we can connect with when we surrender into the God Image within. Notice how different that may be from acting *from* a burdened part that wants to take you over. What a change!

That brings us to the question, What if the firefighter is *in me*? What do I do then?

Situation Number Three:
Oh Dear, Those Little Buggers Are Mine

When the firefighters are ours, we are likely engaged in behaviors that are hurtful, and we often feel ashamed. It's a hard spot in which to find ourselves. But there is an answer.

First, we need to clear up the misconception that if we are "good Christians," we can't or won't have firefighters. According to this belief, a "real Christian" can't struggle with alcoholism, porn addiction, rage, suicidal ideation, or anorexia. All the things we whisper in church because they are too shameful to say out loud.

But the truth is that Christians do have firefighters. Lots of them. One difference between us and the rest of the world might be that we don't always feel permission to speak the truth about them. So, we have firefighters . . . and we lie about them.

Which leaves us feeling alone and apart in our struggle.

Allow me to say to you with great tenderness, you are not your firefighter. Let that sink in to the depths of your soul. Your firefighter is a part of you that is trying to help you in an unhelpful way. But it is not you. You are made in the image of a God who loves you. Your firefighter is just a part of you that needs healing.

Getting Help for a Firefighter

When we have firefighters, we need our support people because most firefighters require a level of professional expertise that we don't have on our own. There's nothing at all wrong with that. It just means that firefighters are entrenched. And they matter. Because in the middle of trying so hard to help, they are probably making a dangerous mess of your life. We'd love to help them find a better way to help, and do so quickly. Before your pain gets a whole heck of a lot worse.

You are not your firefighter.

Whatever your firefighter, please find a therapist, nutritionist, medical facility, or twelve-step group that has that specialization. I promise this makes sense.

If I have a heart problem, I'm not going to my dentist for heart surgery no matter how much I like him. No matter if he's a Christian. I'm going to a cardiovascular surgeon because he's trained and skilled in heart surgery.

The same principle holds true with firefighters. Alcoholic firefighters need addiction specialists. Food firefighters need eating disorder specialists. Sexual Acting Out firefighters need sex addiction specialists.

It just makes sense.

Our firefighters will fight us tooth and nail against seeking that help. They often need the gifts of pain and hitting bottom before our manager parts finally get scared enough to seek support. It's difficult to ask for help. But perhaps you are not reading this book by accident, and maybe you can get help for your firefighters before they take you to a bottom that you don't want to hit.

I invite you—really invite you—to consider that. We who specialize in treating firefighters are great folks. You'll like us. Come give us a try.

Okay, so what does getting help for a firefighter look like?

Well, let's say Joe grew up in a home where he had the experience of being not enough. That exile might have developed in a number of very different possible ways.

Perhaps he had abusive parents who screamed at him or hit him or perpetrated the devastation of sexual abuse.

Perhaps Mom was an alcoholic and spent her evenings with the bottle instead of with him. Or perhaps Mom and Dad divorced when he was young, and Dad took off and checked out.

Perhaps Mom and Dad were a loving Christian couple but had impossible standards that Joe could never meet. The report card with five As and one B was received with shame.

Perhaps Joe had a superhero older sibling who got all of Mom and Dad's attention, and he felt unseen and not valued.

In whatever way it developed, Joe has a real exile that holds his pain, and it started when he was young and without a lot of coping skills. Joe and his buddies went out one night in middle school and got a hold of somebody's parents' stash of beer, and Joe discovered the "answer" to his problems. One drink, and his shame was numbed. He felt confident, on top of the world, the life of the party.

One drink over time led to two and then three because it took more and more to get the same effect. Joe kept drinking on and off through high school, and in college his fraternity experience was one long series of alcoholic binges. Vomiting, hangovers, and blackouts became his regular companions.

The drinking that used to make the pain better was now making it worse. But he couldn't stop.

Graduation and a job helped for a while. He married, had a child, and swore he would cut back on the alcohol. He tried drinking only on weekends, having a glass of water between drinks, not keeping alcohol in the house, switching from vodka to beer, and setting a three-drink limit.

Nothing worked. Sometimes he could go a week, maybe two, without a drink, and then something would happen and he was right back at it. He was powerless over taking that first drink. And once he picked that up, the rest always followed.

Joe is a bright man. He has a great job. His wife adores him, and he seems like a pillar in the community. In his church even. He is strong and accomplished and he can hold his own, even under the influence of so much toxicity in his body. But over time his life slowly unravels.

Firefighters are no respecters of intellect. Or position. Or education. Or anything, really.

Drinks at the business dinner led to behavior he regrets. His wife became distant and critical. His work started to suffer. Then came the first DUI.

There are parts of Joe that are horrified by his behavior. A Spiritualizer part. And of course a Do-It-Right part. These parts are furious with the Alcohol firefighter and regularly yell at it. These parts know Joe's life is deteriorating and the consequences of the drinking are getting worse. Usually, these manager parts take over the morning after a drinking binge: "I've got to stop. I'm not going to drink today. This is crazy. Why do I keep doing this? I'm such an idiot!"

But firefighters are stealthy, folks. Cunning and baffling. They have a sneaky narrative. The firefighter waits a while, until the day has gone on a bit, and then starts to talk to Joe: "I don't have a problem. My drinking is no worse than anyone else's. Tonight it will be different. I'll just have a drink or two with dinner. Just a little something to take the edge off. I don't know what everyone is so worked up about. They are so uptight. I'm fine."

Joe's parts are in an all-out war.

You and I and even a part of Joe know that if the alcoholic part takes full control, he could lose everything. That's because our firefighters are usually way stronger than our managers. They tend to take over more and more completely over time. Unless they have outside support to help them heal.

Joe is dealing with a very serious firefighter. What is the answer? Because you have come this far in the book, you probably know. The answer—for Joe or therapists or pastors or family members—is not to align with his manager part to attack or shame or control the alcoholic part. (That is often ineffective and usually strengthens the drinking.) You probably know the goal is to honor the intent of this hard-working, exhausted, misunderstood, hated part that is trying so hard to help. It needs to be done with boundaries of course. But not shame.

The answer is to comfort the part—and the exile behind it—and bring healing to it so it can stop drinking and be freed to bring something beautiful to his system. Joe needs the support of a skilled addiction specialist, an AA group, and a recovery plan. Absolutely. Without a doubt.

He also needs the wisdom of approaching the therapy, group, and plan with a compassion for the firefighter, not a hatred of it. Not a "Let's kick this firefighter out of the system" kind of approach that has no regard for the pain the firefighter is trying to put out. With that approach he might put down the drink, but he'll have to pick up smoking or eating or another firefighter because the pain is unaddressed.

He needs a *move toward* approach that holds openness, curiosity, and compassion for the drinking part, how it learned to do what it does, and what problem it is trying to solve. Once the part feels heard and respected, it may reveal how exhausted it is, how hard it's been working, and how open it may be to learning that there is a better way to fix the pain. That calling friends in AA is better than picking up a drink. That sharing his struggles is better than isolating.

This approach would invite the part to unblend, to be witnessed, to be loved by his God Image, and to be unburdened. Freed up to do something more helpful than drinking.

Going Deeper: Getting to know a firefighter of my own

Are any firefighters in your own life coming to mind? If so, they are probably fighting tooth and nail to keep you from writing down their names. Of course they are. They don't want to be kicked out. We don't want them to be either.

Take a moment to see if you can just identify a firefighter that you'd like to get to know. Reassure it that you don't want to hurt it or kick it out (the parts of you that want this will need to be invited to step back), you just want to get to know it. Let your awareness just be present with it for a moment. What do you notice about it?

Do you get an image of it, or notice it somewhere in your body as a sensation? Journal what you notice.

Let it know you want to understand how it's trying to help you, and see if it is willing to show you where it learned to try to help you in this way. Journal anything that comes up.

If you feel openness, ask what it's afraid would happen if it didn't do this job for you. Write anything you sense.

If you got the sense that this part of you is afraid you'll be hurt or shamed or rejected in some way, extend appreciation to it for trying to help you avoid those painful possibilities. Notice if it shifts or you observe any changes.

Now you've had a chance to briefly get curious about the motivation of your firefighter. Again, it doesn't make its behavior okay, but it may give you the insight and compassion that you need to help it make real and lasting changes.

WHEN FIREFIGHTERS ARE SLOW TO RESPOND

Yeah. Okay. That sounds great. But what if it doesn't respond? What if it's not that simple?

That's a really good question. A lot of firefighters won't respond, at least at first. In fact, the whole process of unburdening is not a simple one. In therapy, when we first go inward and invite parts to step back, it's common for them to not only refuse, but for multiple protector parts to pile on.

You might wonder, *But don't they know the point is to help?*

No. Quite honestly, they don't. If they did, they probably wouldn't be as stuck in their roles as they are.

The truth is, for most of us new to Spirit-led living, our parts are totally unfamiliar with our God Image. They've honestly never met it before, and they probably don't trust its intentions or its power. Even if we are Christians, because this is a whole different way of relating to God.

We must engage in a process by which the God Image slowly gains experience with the various parts and builds trust by honoring their resistance and asking their permission and hearing their stories. Some parts respond quickly to this respectful attention and find healing quickly. Others—often those more entrenched—take much longer to respond.

Of course, when dealing with dangerous firefighters like Anorexia, Rage, Suicidal/Homicidal Ideation, and Addiction, this needs to be done with a specialist—therapist, nutritionist, maybe law enforcement—who ideally has training in parts work. With actively dangerous parts, external constraints might need to be implemented through means such as restraining orders and separation. Always, safety is the first and primary goal.

But with any part, we will find our most effective way of helping it stop its unhelpful or dangerous behaviors is ultimately not by moving against it, but by moving toward it to understand why it does what it does and what it is afraid will happen if it stops. That opens the door to allowing the God Image to draw near, witness its pain, unburden and release it from the behavior, and allow it to transform into something beautiful.

"Something beautiful" may sound like a stretch to you right now. But I've seen what it can look like many times. The Alcoholic part may bring a quality of restfulness when it is unburdened. The Raging part may bring wise leadership. The Self-Harm part may bring an appreciation for daily living. The Eating part may bring a delight in the complexity and variety of taste and smell.

Each of our parts carry these valuable qualities underneath their firefighter burdens. When we move toward them with compassion and bring healing to their pain, they can be freed to bring something quite beautiful to us as a gift.

They can be as God intended them to be. Unburdened. Set free. Healed and whole.

ALL PARTS WELCOME

Welcome firefighters? Really? I can hear the doubt in your voice. You're thinking clearly now about the damage someone else's firefighter has unloaded all over your life. Or damage you have dumped all over innocent others.

So, am I *sure* we should welcome our firefighters?

My answer is yes, wrapped in thoughtfulness and self-care.

First, the welcome I'm talking about here isn't saying anything goes, or that victims must extend grace or forgiveness without reaching for truth or justice. Rather, it's the freeing awareness that while the behavior the part is engaged in may be harmful, the part itself is well-intentioned and trying its best to help.

Second, when we recognize that amazing truth and can move *toward* our hurting parts with compassion, we will be much more successful in helping them unburden and replace their harmful behavior with helpful behavior. Moving against or away from parts only increases their shame and their pain, and doesn't often change the bad behavior anyway. This is a much more successful way to invite the behavior transformation we hope for and deserve when parts are doing bad things.

And bonus: it's the very essence of Christ.

Take just a minute with that. Think about the thing you do or feel that you are most ashamed of, that you feel most guilty about. That thing you keep doing or feeling even though you swear you are going to stop. Maybe no one in the whole wide world knows about it but you.

Yep—*that* thing. You knew it immediately, even if you didn't want to acknowledge it. Especially if you don't want to acknowledge it.

What if *that* part of you were not just tolerated, not just put up with, but actually *welcomed*, by a holy God who knows it deeply and sees the positive intent behind the behavior it is engaged in?

What if that were really true?

Go ahead and sit with that for a minute.

Because that part has probably never experienced anyone welcoming it. Ever. Yourself included.

I can hear God saying, "C'mere, little part that is coping in this unhelpful way. Tell me what you are afraid would happen if you stopped taking over like this. What problem are you trying to solve? Let me hear your story and comfort you and see if we can find a better way to get to that good goal that you are pursuing. Let me help release you."

I hope you can hear it, too.

Discussion Questions

- What is your favorite example in scripture of Jesus's parts compassion?

- Why might people tend to believe that Christians should not have firefighters? What is flawed about that line of thinking?

- It's often very difficult to separate out the unhelpful behavior of firefighters and their positive intent to help with pain. Why is that? Where do you most struggle with that idea?

- Does it make sense that acknowledging the goal of the firefighter (stopping pain) and helping it see better ways to accomplish that goal is a more effective way to change behavior than hating it or shaming it? If so, why? If not, why is that a challenging concept?

9

UNBURDENED FAITH

Leaving DIY spirituality for the real thing

Spirituality matters. *Really* matters.

The experience and understanding of God in our inner being deeply impacts our relationships, marriages, parenting, careers, finances, sexuality, and even our mental and physical health. When we suffer, it's human to instinctively cry out, "God, help me!" Or, "How could God let this happen?" Somehow, we know deep down that when everything else is stripped away, matters of the spirit remain.

It's strange, then, how often faith turns into the fiercest of war zones. My *History of Religion in America* textbook in grad school was multiple hundreds of pages long. And when I realized it was really one enormous narrative of the hundreds of factions just of Protestantism in the United States, I wanted to cry.

Is this what a loving Creator had in mind for us?

Because you are reading this book, chances are good that you have engaged deeply with spiritual questions. You might be someone who has spent your life in church and identify strongly with a certain denomination or religious practice. Your spiritual life may be vibrant and full, bringing vitality and meaning to your days. You might be someone who used to go to church but began to have questions that didn't have obvious answers, so you slowly drifted from the faith of your childhood.

Perhaps you are someone who has been wounded by a faith community because of a doctrine that was hurtful to your experience, or because of an experience of judgment that felt very unsafe. You may be an agnostic or an atheist who looks at the behavior of "people of faith" and don't see anything in it that reflects a loving God. You may be a curious seeker, earnestly desiring an authentic faith journey and uncertain of the right place to find it. Or you may be someone who was once desperate and hurting and experienced the life-giving refreshment of the divine in your life.

Whatever your unique experience of faith, you deserve to be able to explore and discuss it openly and without judgment or shame. Your experience will look different than mine, and that's beautiful. Your faith journey will be unique to you, mine will be unique to me, and both of our journeys matter. That is why it is important in a book about our inner experience for us to set aside a full chapter of sacred space in which to purposefully explore the role of the divine in our innermost lives. Even though it has been a struggle since the beginning of time to engage in that conversation with respect and honor, all of you and all of me are welcome here.

One of the things that drew me to IFS was that Schwartz's understanding of human nature left room for the spiritual dimension generally while aligning with many Judeo-Christian beliefs specifically. And it offered incredibly helpful solutions that no one I knew was talking about.

With parts awareness, the reasons for spiritual war zones suddenly made sense to me. Perhaps you've already made the connection: We war and fight and faction and splinter because our protectors pile on when they hear words like *belief*, *faith*, *what the Bible says*, or *what God wants for you*. One person leads with a Spiritualizer or Critic while another defends with an Aggressor. A third might chime in with a Thinker/Arguer while a fourth tries to keep the peace with a Caretaker. We argue or shut down and feel judged and rejected and more distant from each other; we get angry, try to control, and eventually give up and walk away in frustration.

Have you ever had experiences like these?

By contrast, we all desire a deeply safe, open, respectful, and warm space to be present with issues that matter most, without fear or judgment, shame or condemnation. A place where we can speak our truth and ask honest questions. Where we are welcome just as we are, with our honest experience and feelings. This is our experience when we are present in the God Image at our core, and it is the beauty and safety that we all seek when we step onto a spiritual path. From this inner core that by its very nature is the seat of genuine spirituality, we experience and also pour out the radiance of God. We know it when we experience it in someone else. We are drawn in, feel seen and heard, feel cared for. We come away blessed by hope.

Now, this Imago Dei—our core God Image—is so powerful, so transformative, that it makes complete sense that we might have a well-intentioned part that attempts to re-create it through effort. Especially if we feel "not good enough" for God, and very much want to please him and "do it right." This part that tries to "do" religion and faith correctly is a familiar friend to me, has played a role in my own faith journey, and has been a part of the faith journeys of many people that I know and love. As you know from chapter 6, I've fondly named this part "Spiritualizer." And Spiritualizer is a wonderful part, just like all our other parts. It may have gotten stuck in some unhelpful ways of behaving, but it's a good part, even if it's trapped in a bad role. Let's not forget that important truth in this difficult conversation. Spiritualizer is exactly like all other burdened protectors. It just tends to evoke more reactivity because it dabbles in the divine. So together we will gently and respectfully get to know this wonderful, challenging, hard-working, earnest part of us that we probably all know, and that we maybe even love.

As its name implies, our Spiritualizer is a high-performing but burdened part that tries earnestly to do religion perfectly. It's the part that tries to replicate or force authentic spirituality, yet it's also where so much of our spiritual confusion originates.

Getting to know it can be difficult because we sometimes so strongly identify with our Spiritualizer part that it can feel indistinguishable from our core Imago Dei. This then blinds us to a larger truth: *Spiritualizer, well intended as it is, behaves like all other burdened protectors. It unwittingly creates the opposite outcome to what it desires. Where it seeks to effect love, it delivers hate. Where it struggles to bring unity, it evokes division. Where it preaches words of grace, it conveys a spirit of condemnation. It has broken families into tiny pieces. It has started wars. Across America today, it is split-ting beautiful communities of faith in two.* And when we can't recognize it, we won't know how to heal it so that our authentic God Image can direct our hearts.

I'm grateful that IFS offers us a powerful first step: the ability to distinguish our Spiritualizer part from the Imago Dei at our core. That awareness alone will change our spiritual lives.

Most of us intuitively connect with the awareness that no recon-ciliation with ourselves, others, or God is possible without authentic spirituality. No genuine flourishing. As folks in recovery circles say, a spiritual problem requires a spiritual solution.

That's what I want to explore next.

GLUE THE TAIL ON THE SHEEP

For many of us, what happens in this most critical area of life is that we are handed a version of faith in our childhoods that we never really grow beyond. Maybe, as I've heard Pastor Andy Stanley of North Point Community Church say, we learned this childhood faith while gluing cotton-ball tails on Bible story sheep at craft time. Later, if we asked hard questions, we might have been given elementary answers that didn't make sense for us. Or maybe we never looked for better answers until life got hard. If in this process we inadvertently developed and confused a well-meaning Spiritualizer part for authentic faith, I'd love to help us come to understand what happened.

Part of the defining characteristic of burdened Spiritualizer parts is that, once formed, they must stay defended against growth and alternate perspectives. They can't be challenged or open in their thinking. They have to think in terms of *us versus them.* That way they know how to tell who's "doing it right." They need to look for difference rather than con-nection, and they feel threatened by people, things, and ways of thinking that are different.

Remember the all-consuming mission of a Spiritualizer part: the

Spiritualizer strives to "do" religion perfectly in order to protect the exile that feels unaccepted by God or others. For this reason, it is very intent on keeping score, depending on black-and-white / right-or-wrong thinking to keep a clear tally of which side of the line we (and therefore, others) fall on.

If we are fully identified with Spiritualizer parts, our options are limited. Open conversations and honest wrestling with uncertainty do not sit well with our hard-working Spiritualizer. We feel that we can only engage with those who share our exact beliefs, and that we must shove down any parts of us that question or struggle. Or we can risk being shamed and judged, wrestle with mature spiritual issues alone, or feel

> *The Spiritualizer strives to "do" religion perfectly in order to protect the exile that feels unaccepted by God or others.*

out of place if we ask questions that challenge our faith community's beliefs. We might even be tempted to believe we've lost our faith if we ask real questions of Spiritualizer parts, because genuine questions feel like a threat to Spiritualizer and it will defend against them.

This is tragic, when you think about it. In school, we are required to think critically, read, and discuss all manner of new and challenging topics that we may or may not agree with or even understand. In our workplaces, we are asked to pursue certifications, continuing education, and training so that we can grow and expand our thinking and avoid becoming stagnant.

But when we have a Spiritualizer part, we become strongly biased against critical thinking in this most crucial area of our lives.

In some circles, even talking about spirituality is taboo.

To make matters worse, most public discourse on matters of spirituality features the extremes of the conversation, such that our skewed perceptions of the opposite viewpoint are reinforced.

"Those crazy liberals are out to end the world with their atheism."

"Those ridiculous conservative evangelicals just hate everyone."

This, too, creates circles of insular thinking that discourage people from thinking rationally or thoughtfully. From growing. From change.

Whole communities and traditions of faith can stay stuck at a glue-the-cotton-ball-on-the-tail-of-the-sheep level spirituality.

Fortunately—and, I'll admit, painfully—life doesn't allow most of us to stay spiritually stuck. I've noticed two primary ways that we bring ourselves to crisis points in our faith journeys: when we are questioning and when we are suffering. The outcome of our crisis depends significantly on whether we encounter a genuine faith—an Imago Dei—or a Spiritualizer.

CRISIS POINT ONE: QUESTIONING

Somewhere along the line, most of us hit a dry season in our faith where no matter what we did, God seemed silent. Can you relate? Maybe your prayers felt like they bounced off the ceiling, and the God who used to feel so real seemed completely AWOL. You began to ask hard questions about God and faith and eternity, because God wasn't showing up in the ways you expected him to, and that was rocking your world.

I sincerely hope that in that moment you encountered someone's God Image. Someone who could sit Immanuel *with* you in your struggle and questions with validation and gentleness and compassion. Without shame. Without "fixing." Just presence. When we meet the authentic divine in another in these painful places, our faith flourishes, our vision of God expands, our ability to be at peace with our suffering increases. Such an experience of God's presence is life giving, faith enhancing, safe, kind.

If you did meet a God Image–led person in this pivotal moment, perhaps they told you about the "dark night of the soul." They may have gently shared with you the writings of suffering saints like St. John of the Cross, who help us understand that this dark night actually is a critical stage of spiritual growth. That it's a developmental period, much like the time when a child is finally allowed to cry himself to sleep at night with the parent standing on the other side of the door, heart breaking at the cries, knowing the child cannot mature if he cannot move through the stage of having parents soothe him in the middle of the night.

You may have felt great relief to discover that you should *expect* to walk through a dark night of the soul if you are growing spiritually, and that not only is it *not* an indication that you are failing spiritually, it is actually a sign that you are growing appropriately. That you cannot mature in your faith if you don't go through this spiritual milestone. Perhaps even go through it more than once. And if you did encounter a God Image–led person such as this, you probably left the conversation feeling deeply seen, safely known, and intimately encouraged. Closer to God.

Now, a Spiritualizer also wants to "do it right" when it responds to your dark night. However, it will be so focused on fixing and performance that if you had the courage to share your experience honestly with a Spiritualizer, you might have been offered religious platitudes and advice about what you were doing wrong or needed to do differently to get God to "show up."

Pray more.

Fast.

Read this section of scripture.

Do that Bible study.

Or even more heartbreakingly, perhaps you were accused of being "in sin" as an explanation of why God was "punishing" you by withdrawing his presence. Because of his displeasure with your poor spiritual performance. This is the experience of the Spiritualizer. Judgment. Critique. Unsolicited advice. Condemnation. With a burdened agenda to get us to "do it right." Why? Because a Spiritualizer's job is to eliminate mess and pain.

Sadly, the collateral damage from an eager Spiritualizer is significant. It causes us to pretend and to hide. It unintentionally hurts you and hurts me. And it drives us away from the God who sees because we become desperately afraid of just exactly what he will see when he looks inside.

Cotton-ball faith is a happy place to start, but it is no way to flourish after we graduate from kid's church. Cotton-ball spirituality follows a formula:

Thinking right thoughts
+ Doing right things
= God shows up in a way that feels good
and real and makes everything better.

Spiritualizer parts rely on that kind of fixed, transactional theology. But genuine spirituality thrives on a different currency. Our God Image– experience of faith has a much more expansive perspective that allows God to be God on his terms. It holds no judgment for our real and often painful feelings about the difference between his terms and ours.

The God Image within us knows and accepts that it hurts to have honest and sincere prayers seem to bounce off the ceiling. Because it's a human thing. Even a Jesus thing.[49] And there's no shame in that.

CRISIS POINT TWO: SUFFERING

When it comes to pain, we desperately want to know we are not alone. It doesn't really matter what kind of pain it is—cancer, job loss, infidelity, barrenness, moving, death. We just need to know our actual experience is normal, and that it's okay to feel what we are feeling. We need Immanuel. God *with* us. That's why when we suffer, we gravitate to God Image–led people. We long to be received as we truly are, especially when we feel alone. The God Image in another will be present with us in our suffering. With deep compassion and connection, without agenda, without the need to fix or advise. It is the flesh-and-bones God presence that we need when we are in pain. We are deeply healed when surrounded in our hurt and shame by the quiet, loving presence of a compassionate other. Deep calls to deep. This was Jesus.

We can endure anything when we are seen, really seen, and known and held. This is the grace of the God Image—a *being with* in love and compassion. Immanuel. This is the very essence of God-with-us. God with us as we are with one another. It is the very opposite of Spiritual- izing, which is a separating, isolating, shaming encounter. Our suffering is profoundly compounded when we have to bottle it up and say we are "fine" and not ask for help, comfort, or community because we fear being met with the judgment, shame, or unsolicited advice of a Spiritualizer. It's critical that we understand the difference between these two, because while they both may use God language, one reflects the Divine and the other reflects the Destroyer. I don't know about you, but I want to be on the side of the Divine.

Consider the Jewish practice of sitting *shiva* with those who grieve.

To me, it provides a beautiful picture of what "being with" in our God Image–led selves can look like in practice.

The Hebrew word *shiva* literally means *seven*, and reflects one of the formal stages of mourning that the Jewish community observes after the loss of a loved one. In contemporary shiva people sit on short boxes to represent being brought low in their grief. In biblical times they sat on the ground. In ashes, even. Back then people didn't hide their grief. They felt their fear and expressed their sorrow when bad things happened. Outwardly showed it and inwardly felt it. They tore their clothes and put ashes on their heads, as if to say, "My heart has turned to ashes and feels burned up." Then they sat in the ashes for seven days and allowed themselves to experience the grief. It was a round-the-clock investment in getting the grief out and being honest with the pain—a little different than our typical modern, "Fine, I'm fine. I'm doing okay."

We who live in contemporary America could learn so much from just that act of honesty. But amazingly, it gets even better.

Lo and behold, family and friends would join them in their grief, silently sitting in the ashes with the hurting person. By simply being with the hurting person, they would embody God Image–reverence for the pain and the process of suffering.

No judgment. No advice. No well-meaning but super-painful Spiritualizer comments: "Well, God must have needed her more than you do." Or, "God won't give you more than you can handle, so this suffering must really be God's vote of confidence in you." Or, "Have you gotten away from God that this has happened to you?"

There are none of those unintentionally hurtful things people say when they are trying to help but have Spiritualizer parts that are uncomfortable and don't know how to sit with grief.

In shiva, it is the mourner, and only the mourner, who can break the silence. Who can speak first. Who can break the sanctity of silence with the somehow incompleteness of words.

Remember Job's friends? They brought their God Image to Job's suffering while sitting shiva with him. Sitting silently in the ashes in his deepest pain and grief. But then they opened their mouths and their Spiritualizers started talking. And that was the pivot where they went from healing to wounding, from helpful to hurtful, from honoring God to playing God. And God was not pleased.

GROWTH REQUIRES CHANGE

Once we recognize that there's a world of difference between Spiritualizer and our spiritual core, we must wrap our minds around the concept of real, authentic spiritual growth. What is it? How does it happen?

Right off the bat, can we agree that growth requires change? And can we also agree that change, for most of us, isn't easy?

My kids know this in spades. They both experienced pretty significant growing pains in their adolescent years. Which sounds kind of cute until you have a child up in the middle of the night with pain in their legs that a painkiller really doesn't touch.

Why does this happen? Well, their bones are changing. Their bodies are transforming from a child into an adult. That's a lot of growing, and growth hurts.

I used to be able to hold my kids in my arms, and now they tower over me. In fact, at five foot nine, I am by far the shortest person in my family. The kids passed me years ago. It's kind of funny when you are looking *up* at a child while you try to parent.

So, if it is true that spiritual growth necessarily involves change, why do our Spiritualizer parts react so adversely to it?

Let me ask: has your way of thinking about a spiritual issue ever changed? Even slightly? By that I mean did you start with one perspective on a spiritual topic, re-evaluate it in light of new thinking or new awareness, and then arrive at a different perspective?

This is called critical thinking. It leads to more sophisticated, personalized thought processes and more mature belief structures. It is what allows any of us to reach our fullest spiritual, emotional, and intellectual potential. This is also how the faith of our parents becomes a faith of our own.

We can do this in our authentic spiritual self. Not so much in burdened Spiritualizer parts.

For growth to happen we need have permission and space to consider another alternative than the one we currently hold. This is the invitation Jesus offered to the Pharisees. To see the beauty of the divine right in front of them, even when it differed radically from the rules their Spiritualizers had constructed.

Listening with curiosity doesn't mean we are throwing out our faith. It means we are being fully attentive to a matter of great importance. And holding space that it might possibly contain a truth that we hadn't considered before.

THE M&M'S PROOF

Let's go back to math for a moment. I believe with all my heart that 3 + 3 = 6. I know this to be Truth because in elementary school someone taught me that 3 + 3 = 6, and I counted three M&M's, added three more M&M's, and arrived at the grand total of six M&M's. When I ate three of those M&M's, I reverse-proofed the mathematic formula because it turns out that six M&M's minus three M&M's is actually three M&M's. (Minus three more M&M's is actually zero M&M's, but let's not mention that.)

Over the course of my life, I've experienced this Truth to be true in many, many, different ways, such that deep in my soul I just k-n-o-w that 3 + 3 = 6, and if you try to convince me otherwise I will not be changed in my belief.

Am I threatened and defensive if you suggest that 2 + 2 = 6? Nope. Not at all.

Why can I stay open to that conversation while not being threatened in my belief about 3 + 3? Because Truth doesn't change, so I don't need to be afraid to examine it.

I am not the least bit worried about engaging in a wholehearted conversation about 2 + 2, because I know if I openly explore that possibility and add two M&M's to two M&M's, I will not arrive at 6. However, if I *did* arrive at 6 when adding 2 + 2, I would actually want to know about that, because that would mean my current perspective on 3 + 3 was not the whole picture. Or my reasoning skills were flawed. And either way, I'd be better off for having explored it thoughtfully. I'd be closer to the actual Truth.

We can understand with chocolate what is harder to see with faith: that having an open mind is not a threatening proposition. Unless I'm afraid of Truth.

If Truth is Truth, we should have complete comfort in open-mindedly exploring it, because the only two things that can happen are (1) my awareness of the Truth I hold will be reinforced, or (2) my understanding of Truth will expand to be more complete than that which I currently know.

Because Truth doesn't change, I don't need to be afraid to examine it.

This does, of course, require that I acknowledge I might not at present know everything absolutely perfectly.

Ahem.

That can be hard, and our Spiritualizer parts don't like it one bit. Still, my perspective on some spiritual topics has changed or expanded over the course of my faith journey. Maybe yours have, too.

HOLY YOGA

I used to bristle about stuff like yoga and meditation. I had been taught that those things were heretical, and that if I participated in those activities my faith would be in serious jeopardy.

Now, I didn't have any understanding of yoga or meditation. They were just outside any experience I'd had, and my Spiritualizer was determined not to get near those scary, "heretical" things. And then I began to realize that meditation is something God actually invites me to do.

"Whatever is true, whatever is noble, whatever is right, whatever is pure . . . *think about* such things."[50]

"Keep this Book of the Law always on your lips; *meditate* on it day and night."[51]

"Blessed is the one . . . whose delight is in the law of the LORD, and who *meditates* on his law day and night."[52]

A meditative practice is really just a quieting of the mind so I can focus on things of higher value. Not a problem. Nothing threatening about that at all.

Turns out I can also participate in the beneficial physical aspects of yoga without being threatened by religious concepts that might not be consistent with my faith. I have found that by experiencing the mindfulness that yoga invites, I can learn to be a more loving and present person in a way that is completely consistent with the heart of a loving God

Did you know that the yoga term "Namaste" means "I bow to/honor the God Image within you"? Which is another way of saying, "No matter what crazy stuff your parts are doing, I see and know that who you really are is your God Image, and I honor that deep God-presence within you."

The practice of mindfulness and meditation, which calms the mind and body and therefore helps burdened parts to relax, actually gives me greater access to the core of my being. Other traditions call it *flow* or *centeredness*, but I call it prayer.

You might name other experiences that rise to the level of a spiritual practice. For you, it might be running, spending time in nature or your garden, immersing yourself in music, or the hours you put in serving at your local soup kitchen. If so, you'll understand me when I say that in some very tangible ways, yoga and meditation have helped me live out my Christian faith in more genuine ways than my Spiritualizing parts were ever able to.

SAME BIBLE, NEW INSIGHT

When we invite old problems to meet new thoughts and experiences, our growing understandings can also include specifics of theology. Our authentic spiritual core will be curious and open to these new growing revelations. Our Spiritualizer parts will be threatened by them. For example, I have always heard it taught that Adam and Eve were cast out of the Garden of Eden after they ate the forbidden fruit as God's divine punishment for their sinning.

In essence, I read that as God saying, "Hey, I caught you being naughty. You're gonna pay for that." Then he booted their sorry selves out of paradise so they would suffer for their naughtiness (and their kids would, and the next umpteen generations of people in the whole history of the world would, too, because God is super vindictive like that).

At least that was my takeaway. That was my cotton-ball explanation, and it followed me into my adult faith. Then I went to graduate school and took theology classes from really smart people. One of my professors pointed out a sentence in Genesis 3 that I had never noticed before.

"And the Lord God said, 'The man has now become like one of us, knowing good and evil. He must not be allowed to reach out his hand and take also from the tree of life and eat, and live forever.'"[53]

Because mankind now carried the DNA of sin, he explained, it would have actually been torture to never be able to die and escape this world of sin and pain and suffering. In other words, being cast out of the garden was actually protection, not punishment.

Whoa. A whole new perspective. And a pretty big theological shift, because it says a lot about how God relates to us in our sin. Which is in a way that feels a whole lot more loving than my original understanding.

Or take that terrible scene of suffering on the cross. At three in the afternoon Jesus cried out in a loud voice, *"Eloi, Eloi, lema sabachthani?"* ("My God, my God, why have you forsaken me?")[54]

My cotton-ball version of this pivotal event in history was something along the lines of, "God is pure and holy, and he cannot stand the presence of evil. So when evil was fully resting on Jesus, God had to turn his face away, even from his only Son."

Which makes sense until you really start to think about it. I recall a scene in Job chapter 1. Satan himself is hanging out in God's throne room with none other than the living God, having a face-to-face conversation. That shoots down the whole God-can't-be-in-the-presence-of-evil argument because he didn't object to a visit from Satan, the ultrabomb of evilness.

If God was fully present with Christ on the cross, what is the meaning of Jesus's heart-rending cry of abandonment?

I've given this a lot of thought and prayer. One day it occurred to me that one side effect of sin is that it causes us to *feel* like we are alone. Like God has turned his back on us.

Sin makes it *feel* like God has abandoned us, even though he hasn't.

In clinical language, we call that an *attachment wound.*

If I understand correctly, God is way bigger than sin, than evil, than wickedness. Not only can he stand in the presence of it, he even supersedes it. He is present always—the divine quality of omnipresence—even when it doesn't seem like he is. And Jesus, because he was fully human in addition to being fully God, was giving expression to the felt experience of abandonment, not the actual reality of it.

I'm describing this line of thinking for you to show how a person's beliefs can shift and develop depth. Now, I don't present myself as a theologian, and I don't play one on TV, so please don't take anything I say as gospel truth.

What I am saying is that if I rigidly refuse to consider any thought, feeling, or perspective other than the one I currently hold, my thinking and spiritual development will be truncated. My Spiritualizer may be happy, but I will stay stuck in cotton-ball faith.

Spiritualizing parts are closed. Our God Image is open, connected, curious, clear-minded. This is where growth occurs.

This is why if you grew up in a faith environment that was closed and didn't encourage critical thinking, and then went to college and heard other perspectives for the first time, you may have been tempted to jettison your faith altogether. You hadn't been able to develop the God Image skills to take in new opinions and think wisely and thoughtfully. During my first week of college, my intro to philosophy professor put up a three-point logic proof on the board that clearly evidenced that God could not exist. In a one-hour class, I almost lost the spiritual legacy of my previous eighteen years.

All that don't-talk-about-anything-that-isn't-exactly-in-the-box-of-what-we-believe had gotten me to a cotton-ball level of faith. No adult thinking skills required.

> *Spiritualizing parts are closed. Our God Image is open, connected, curious, clear-minded.*

Jesus talked a lot about how rigid beliefs can actually block our ability to see God in the now. In John 5:39–40, we read, "You study the Scriptures diligently because you think that in them you have eternal life. These are the very Scriptures that testify about me, yet you refuse to come to me to have life."

In other words, "Guys, look up from the rules! Get out of your own best thinking! The ideas you are holding on to as Truth are not the whole Truth. You are missing the only Truth that matters because you refuse to open your minds to other possibilities. You are missing me!"

That is exactly what our well-intentioned Spiritualizer manager parts do. They hang on to thoughts or beliefs about God or Jesus or religion or spirituality that are closed. That are threatened by outside perspectives. They move against other ways of thinking—by calling them heresy, by condemning people who hold those other beliefs, or by all manner of other hurtful things that sound like faith but may not reflect a loving and mature heart of God.

DOUBLE BINDS

As we are growing in our ability to discern between authentic spirituality and Spiritualizer parts, it's helpful to notice the sticky experience of double binds.

A double bind is a lose-lose situation. Darned if you do. Also darned if you don't.

For our God Image, our authentic connection with the divine, this is never an issue. Our "yes" is our "yes" and our "no" is our "no." We mean what we say and we say what we mean. When we are fully connected to our God Image core, you can trust our words because they will always be honest.

Unfortunately, the double bind is a hallmark of a Spiritualizer manager. It doesn't mean to, you understand, but that's the natural outcome of its well-intentioned behavior. Spiritualizers say one thing and mean another, and the result is deep confusion.

This is a classic experience in unhealthy families. Let's say Dad is an alcoholic and likes to drink—a *lot*—after work. Let's say little Suzy-Q comes in from playing outside and sees her dad passed out on the couch, reeking of beer, and says "Mommy, what's wrong with Daddy?" Mommy, wanting to protect her child from the truth that is inescapable, says, "Nothing, Daddy's just sick." Or, "Daddy's sleeping."

So here you have the double bind. Suzy-Q knows, or will come to know, that Daddy is not sick or sleeping. She's probably smelled beer on him many times before, and she knows he's not okay. But Mommy is saying everything's okay when everything is *not* okay, and now Suzy is in a double bind. She can either trust her inner sense of truth and therefore have to believe that Mommy is lying (which she is), or disregard her own knowing in order to believe that Mommy is not a liar (in addition to

Daddy being an alcoholic). That's a double bind. You either can't believe your own truth or you can't believe your parent's truth.

Lose-lose.

Unfortunately, burdened communities do the same thing as burdened families: say one thing and do another. Maybe we preach the words of grace but we live out judgment. We teach, "There is nothing you can do to make God love you any more or any less," but the unspoken truth is that people are not safe to share their deepest struggles or even negative emotions (like fear, shame, or pride) for fear of being judged and shamed by others, and therefore (it seems) by God.

That's a double bind. I am expected to believe—or say I believe—one thing (grace) but live as though another is true (works/performance/judgment/shame). It's crazy making. Just like the alcoholic family.

Interestingly, although our Spiritualizer parts are the ones creating this double bind, they are also the ones trying to protect us from it.

Our Spiritualizer parts know scripture inside and out. They know that scripture teaches grace. They say all the right things, and they really, really want to believe those things. Take, "For it is by grace you have been saved, through faith—and this is not from yourselves, it is the gift of God—not by works, so that no one can boast."[55] No one in a Christian congregation that I've ever sat in would debate that. We all nod our heads and say, "Yep, grace alone. There's nothing I can do to earn God's favor."

Our God Image intuitively knows and experiences these truths at a deep level. How would we know?

Perhaps you've had moments when you have connected deeply, at an experiential level, with God's radical, loving acceptance of you. With your God Image. Maybe at a youth retreat or a Bible study retreat or Christian men's or women's conference. And it was emotional. You felt it. You wept. It moved you. Then you came back into "real life," speaking those same words of grace, but maybe you were jarred by your experience that those words of grace and unconditional acceptance weren't a felt reality in your community. So, your Spiritualizer part armored up to protect you from judgment and shame.

Our Spiritualizer parts carry the fear of the double bind, that they should believe in grace but they must make us "do it right" or we will somehow disappoint God, or worse, provoke his wrath or the judgment of his people. Toward this end, they struggle and perform and lie to make us feel, say, and do the right things, even if those things aren't congruent for us.

> Authentic spirituality is entirely unburdened. Free. Deep. Rich. Connected to deep communion with God.

Remember, a key difference between authentic spirituality and a Spiritualizer part is that the part is burdened and stuck in an unhelpful role, trying to protect an exile that feels not good enough: that feels broken, worthless, or stupid. Authentic spirituality is entirely unburdened. Free, deep, rich. Connected to communion with God at a deep and resonant level. It is not an effort, but an abandon.

HIERARCHY OF SIN: THE HOLY TAPE MEASURE

Another key indicator differentiating authentic spirituality from a Spiritualizer is the Holy Tape Measure. Spiritualizer has one. God Image does not. For a Spiritualizer, a tape measure is essential, because a ruler of some sort is needed to quantify "badness." Spiritualizer needs to know how "bad" we are to make us be "good-er" so we can pass muster with the Big Guy.

So it builds a hierarchy of sin: Not-so-Bad, Badder, and Baddest. Then it can tell just how bad we are compared to the guy next to us. And because it earnestly wants us (and others) to be "good-er" enough for God, it will level intense vitriol against "those people" who struggle with "those Baddest sins." Or it may inflict a violent amount of spiritual self-hatred if we happen to be one of "those people" and it's afraid we will be unacceptable to God if we have a Baddest sin in our life.

When my Spiritualizer is in charge, if I don't happen to struggle with the particular sin being railed against, I will tend to feel self-righteous about my own lack of struggle in that area and either condemn or feel superior to those who do. But I also come away with a clear felt experience that the sins I do struggle with had better not ever come to light, or that same level of condemnation will land on me. It creates fear that the minute my vulnerability is exposed, you'll go for the jugular. I'm not safe. And then, sadly, we come to believe we are not safe with God either.

That's the polar opposite experience of our authentic spirituality. Our God Image knows that we all have burdened parts, understands that they all separate us from the divine within us and others, and holds deep compassion and sorrow for that reality. It overflows with love and tenderness for the heartache that caused our parts to burden in the first place, not from a place of pity or sympathy (me up here, you down there), but with genuine empathy that knows that my burdened parts are as painful as yours, regardless of what they are each doing. It genuinely reflects the equitability of scripture's grouping of sin: "The acts of the flesh [sinful nature] are obvious: sexual immorality, impurity and debauchery; idolatry and witchcraft; hatred, discord, jealousy, fits of rage, selfish ambition, dissensions, factions and envy; drunkenness, orgies, and the like."[56]

Selfishness and jealousy fall into the same list as orgies and witchcraft. Different flavors of exactly the same sin nature. Just the predictable behavior of burdened parts, separating us from God. From the God Image within.

Remember the Pharisees who wanted to kill the woman in adultery? They had her adultery in a "worse than" category than their self-righteous aggrandizement. Than their spiritual narcissism. But Jesus looked their Spiritualizer parts in the eye and said gently "cast the first stone." And then turned to the woman and said, "Neither do I condemn you." To both the message was tender, loving, and instructive. *You have been met with grace. Now go and sin no more.*[57]

WHO'S RUNNING THE SHOW?

In this chapter we've highlighted a number of differences between authentic spirituality and a Spiritualizer part. It may be helpful to have a quick compare-and-contrast list to review.

Spiritualizer Characteristics

- Stuck in a burdened role (spiritual striving) to try to prevent the pain of an exile from being activated
- Focused on "doing" spirituality perfectly, because it fears God is punishing
- Uncomfortable with negative feelings (sadness, anger, resentment, fear, anxiety, insecurity)
- Closed, defended, and defensive against unfamiliar ways of thinking about spirituality
- Has an agenda: gives unsolicited advice, emotionally unsafe
- Sees sin in a hierarchy and holds a Holy Tape Measure to keep score
- Perceives the world in terms of "us" versus "them"
- Appearance- and performance-oriented, rule-based
- Driven by fear of failure, rejection, judgment, lack of control, abandonment
- Black-and-white / all-or-nothing thinking
- Says one thing (love/grace), feels another (judgment/shame/pressure to perform and/or control)
- Creates double binds
- Lives with a painful disconnect between what is presented to the world on the outside and what is true inside
- Unintentionally rigid, striving, judging, shaming, divisive, wounding

God Image Characteristics

- An unburdened, free-flowing, natural expression of the divine within each human being
- Surrendered rather than striving
- Deeply comfortable with the imperfect journey of being human
- Able to genuinely welcome the full range of human emotions
- Clear, calm, settled experience of Truth
- Open, respectful, free from any agenda to "fix" another

- Understands that sin, or burdens, are anything that separates us from God
- Sees the God Image in every human: thinks in terms of *we*
- Focused on being and present to life
- Heart-oriented
- Overflow of love, compassion, grace
- Emotionally safe, empathic, authentic, sincere
- Sees the whole picture, embraces complexity
- Words and actions are congruent
- Flexible
- Healing

If you, like me, recognize some of the traits of Spiritualizer in your life, I invite you to be gentle and gracious with them. We are in good company. Saul had to come to terms with his Spiritualizer too. But after he repented (changed his mind and went in the opposite direction of his spiritualizing, toward authentic faith), God used him to change the world. You and I have probably been deeply influenced by the writings of this man who exchanged his DIY spirituality for the real thing. So take heart. I know it isn't always easy. If you are into Monty Python at all, you may recall:

"Buuurn her! She's a witch!"
"I'm not a witch! They dressed me up like this."
[Guilty looks.]
"Well, we did do the nose. And the hat. But she is a witch."

We'd really like to find the right "witch to burn" so we can get on with "doing our churching right." Instead, let's move toward that hard-working Spiritualizer with grace and compassion that is gentle and curious about how it came to be, how it feels about the job it's doing, and what it fears will happen if it stops. It needs to know there's a gracious Imago Dei inside waiting to release it from its burdens.

GETTING TO KNOW A SPIRITUALIZER

We've covered a lot in this chapter, and if we have a Spiritualizer part (most of us do), it may be agitated. I get that. We want it to know how much it is valued and get to know and appreciate all the ways it is trying to help us. We want it to know that we understand its positive intentions. Let's take a minute to do that.

Allow me to encourage you again to not just read what follows but to experience it. Thoughtfully. Patiently. Personally. And journal whatever you notice at each step. You, my friend, are worth nothing less!

Going Deeper: Getting to know a Spiritualizer

Take a moment and settle into a quiet space, free of distractions. Take a couple of deep breaths and begin to settle into your body and draw your awareness to what is coming up for you right now. If you are feeling defensive, agitated, angry, or threatened, that could be a Spiritualizer part that is activated. Just warmly notice whatever is there. Even if you aren't aware of it being activated, you can invite your Spiritualizer to interact with you.

Journal whatever you notice.

When it is present, where do you feel it in your body?

Is it willing to show you an image of itself?

Describe how you see this part.

Now, do a brief Spiritual MRI. Notice how you are feeling *toward* the Spiritualizer part. You may very well have parts that feel angry or frustrated with it, or perhaps protective and defensive of it. Welcome anything you notice and ask those parts if they would allow you space to be present with your Spiritualizer (without other parts blended) so you can get to know it. Your Spiritualizer won't be able to interact in helpful ways with you until the other parts have stepped back.

Are you aware of other parts that have feelings about Spiritualizer?

What parts are they?

Are they willing to unblend?

When you notice that you feel openhearted toward Spiritualizer, ask if it would be willing to show you how it came to be. Journal what you notice.

Where did it learn to help you in the way it is trying to help you?

What is it afraid would happen if it stopped doing what it does?

What wounded parts of you is it working to protect?

How does it feel about the job it is doing for you?

Is there anything else it would prefer to be doing for you, if it didn't have to Spiritualize?

When you've spent as much time as you'd like getting to know your Spiritualizer, thank it for showing itself to you today, and let it know how much you appreciate how hard it's working to try to help you. Then take a couple of deep breaths and slowly turn your attention back to the room around you.

GREATER COMPASSION, GREATER INSIGHT

When we ask these simple questions of our parts, we can learn quite a lot as they communicate their stories with us in various ways. We might have flashes of memories, or we might get a sense or impression of a word or phrase. We might, in our mind's eye, visualize other parts they are protecting, or those with which they are at war.

Regardless of how our parts communicate with us, we walk away with greater compassion and insight for why they are doing what they are doing. We discover more options for how to get to the goal more effectively and gain increased trust in our internal system that our God Image is actually our most reliable leader.

And what is the goal? Living from our spiritual essence. Authentic faith. Overflowing God.

Discussion Questions

- Do you notice any ways in which you may have been carrying cotton-ball faith?

- If you have ever had a God Image–experience, describe what that was like for you. How did you know your heart was safe and loved? If you have not, what is it like to consider that it is possible?

- Have you ever had someone figuratively sit shiva with you: being with you in your suffering with no judgment and no agenda? If so, how did that impact you?

- Have you ever been impacted by the idea of a hierarchy of sin? Were you on the receiving end of judgment as a result? If so, what was that experience like for you? How did it affect your desire to connect with God?

- Do you identify with the positive motives of a Spiritualizer part? If so, how can you be grateful toward the way it has been trying to help you with your faith?

Part Two

This Changes Everything

*Transforming our relationships with
ourselves, others & God*

10

NEW LENSES

Once we have them, there's no going back

Well, this has been quite a road we've traveled together, hasn't it? Thank you for coming on this journey with me. What a privilege to spend these chapters together exploring a new way of seeing the world.

For most of us, this world of parts is an entirely different way of relating to ourselves and others. In some ways, it is simple (Self, exiles, managers). In other ways, it is radically complex.

Getting a whole new perspective on things reminds me of my recent experience selling our home.

I always liked my home. It was cozy, and, well, so what if we'd had our furniture for the entire twenty-three years since we'd gotten married. I thought it was great then, and I really hadn't looked at it much since. It was just our stuff. You know.

I had my 1995 lenses on.

So when we put our house on the market, we sat back and waited for the lucky potential buyers to gush their rave reviews. Their responses were, umm, consistent. "This house is dated."

Excuse me, but I believe you meant to say our house is lovely. Or homey. Or cute. Or anything else but . . . dated.

I couldn't understand.

That is, until the stager arrived. The stager whisked in with a sympathetic smile and in all of three minutes had the entire house reworked. I don't mean rearranged. I mean *reworked.*

And stumbling awkwardly behind her, scribbling down paint colors and furniture placements, I . . . suddenly . . . began . . . to . . . see. With 2019 lenses.

My house *was* dated. Dark carpet with gold, swirly patterns and plastic greenery in the bookcases. Oh, people. I suddenly began to shrink in embarrassment that I'd ever had anyone over, much less invited buyers in to see *this*.

But think about it: nothing had physically changed while the stager was with me. My carpet was the same as it had been the hour before. Same couch with the same pillows. Same paint colors and artwork and curtains. But what I had seen contentedly through my 1995 lenses now demanded a different response.

The stager had slipped me 2019 glasses, and I could never go back.

It hurt. I was embarrassed that I hadn't seen it this way before. I swallowed my wounded pride, embraced this shift in perspective, and made the changes I needed to make.

We live in a new (to us) house now—sleek and modern. And you can consider this your official invitation to come over for dinner. Search as you might, you will not find a single inch of plastic ivy on any bookshelf.

And the dark carpet with the gold, swirly patterns that I once thought so elegant is now a neutral sisal. Whatever sisal even is.

When we pick up Internal Family Systems, we similarly get to change how we see our life. To look through different lenses at the exact same feelings, behaviors, and thoughts inside us (and others), only now with compassion and respect for these hard-working parts trying to help us. What a relief.

No judgment.

No shaming.

No self-condemnation.

Those feelings and thoughts and behaviors are not who I am, or who you are. They are not my God Image or yours—just parts of us that have taken over for a moment for some really good reasons. Parts of us that are trying to help us with pain.

For me, just the act of slipping on these new lenses bumps my self-compassion and grace for others waaaaaaay up. Especially knowing that Waze still says, "You have arrived" when I type in "God."

And I can breathe a little deeper.

My hope is that you can say the same. In chapter 1, I promised that parts knowledge would help you in every area of life. I told you it can change how we relate with ourselves, with others, and with God. Even how we relate to other groups and cultures.

In the remaining chapters, I will take you through some real-world exercises to prove it. If you've done the exercises in the preceding chapters, you now have experience applying your newfound parts awareness to get to know your exiles, managers, and firefighters. From here on, we bring your new insights and attitudes together to establish a new way of thinking and feeling.

Give yourself plenty of time for these chapters. Reflecting on our own internal systems and exploring new possibilities take time and energy. Resist the inclination to set any particular time frame for this. Look at part 2 of this book as something to fill in at your own pace, a template to return to time and again as you grow in parts awareness and new patterns emerge.

Discussion Question

- In which area of your life would you most like to grow: relating to yourself, to God, to others, or to other groups and cultures?

11

RELATING MORE
EFFECTIVELY: ME TO ME

All parts are truly welcome

Parts awareness allows us to relate much more successfully to ourselves. It gives us self-compassion, healing from unhelpful patterns, and the ability to experience our core spirituality in action. It helps us understand our pain and our triggers, and find more helpful ways to cope. It shows us how to get our needs met in healthy, effective ways so that we can show up in our lives and our world with our best, most authentic selves. Leading with love. Including love for your "misbehaving" parts, because . . . all parts of you are welcome.

I'm hoping by now this is a mantra for you: All parts are truly welcome, because there are no bad parts, only bad roles. But just so we don't become numbed by repetition to the truth that all parts of us are well-intentioned (trying to help), even if what they are doing is not helpful, let's remember why this is actually true.

This is true, I would suggest, because when all parts are welcome, we are doing inside of ourselves what Jesus did on the outside. We are living the love that Jesus called us to and modeled for us. He didn't show up to judge us, shame us, or condemn us. He showed up to save us through an unimaginable act of love. He moved *toward* people with compassion and grace. He embraced the children, the sick, the outcast, the unlovable, the thieves, the tax collectors. Even those who crucified him. He really, truly embraced them. Were they doing good stuff? No. But Jesus's way to bring change to their hearts and actions was to welcome them home.

All parts of you are welcome.

Think of how radically different your life will be when you truly believe and live as though every single part of you is welcome. Is well-intentioned. Is authentically loved by you.

That includes the parts that you've most often despised or tried to keep hidden. The part that compulsively looks at porn. The part that eats the whole bag of Oreos. The part that gossips. That part that rescues. The part that floods you with anxiety and fear. The part that says lots of spiritual stuff and doesn't really feel most of it. The part that covets what your neighbor has and wants your enemies to suffer. The part that shoots up. The part that has suffered abuse and even the part that perpetrates abuse. That rages. That rescues. That cuts or wants to hurt you. That can't stop saying yes until you are saying no to the things that really matter.

All those parts. Welcome. Not just tolerated, but warmly welcomed.

Breathe that reality in for a moment. Isn't that amazing? Did you feel your shoulders drop, your breathing deepen, a sense of relief flood in?

What you know now is that when your God Image can approach these parts with curiosity, love, and compassion, they can be understood, witnessed, healed, and freed up to do something much more helpful in your internal system. They can stop raging, eating, cutting, abusing, gossiping, hating. Not because they are bad at heart, but because they deserve to be freed up to do what they are truly trying to do: help you.

Going Deeper: A me-to-me exercise

Before we begin taking parts awareness into our relationships with the world, let's start with a personal inventory.

How would you most like to use the concepts you've encountered in this book with your parts? Which exiles most need your love and care? Which managers are exhausted and need the most relief? Which firefighters are you afraid to even acknowledge that you have?

Exiles

The inventory that follows will help you process what you're learning. Take a moment to write down the parts of you that you would like to relate more effectively with. Which of your exiles are carrying the most pain? Flood you most easily? Would you most like to see healed?

- Shame
- Anxiety
- Panic
- Fear/Terror
- Self-Doubt
- Self-Loathing
- Sadness
- Depression
- Worthlessness
- Dependency
- Loneliness
- Overwhelmed
- Powerlessness
- Other:

What will your next step(s) be? Be specific and concrete. Use the resources page at the back of the book to create your plan.

Managers

Now, which of your managers are coping in the most unhelpful ways? Know that many managers are hard to detect, because their coping strategies come with some rewards. People like us. We do things well. We get things done. You can tell a burdened manager, however, if it is trying to prevent pain. It worries that if it stops doing its job, there may be a negative outcome (feeling less-than, ashamed, rejected).

There are, of course, many more managers than I've listed here, and you will only truly know your own when you turn your attention inside yourself and meet them. (As you may have suspected by now, some protectors can be either managers or firefighters, depending on whether they jump in to prevent or to put out the pain. Their behavior might be the same, but their timing defines their part.) For now, mark the ones you may have that you'd most like to understand better:

- Perfectionist/Do-It-Right
- Doer
- Thinker
- People Pleaser/Server
- Rescuer
- Self-Critic
- Judge
- Pessimist
- Passive
- Blamer
- Controller

- Busyness
- Don't Talk About It
- Don't Feel It
- Other:

With these wonderful managers, what will your next step(s) be? Be specific and concrete. Review the resources page to add support to your ideas.

Firefighters

And finally, firefighters—those old and secret friends we often want to hide, even from ourselves. With the love of your Imago Dei, you can be compassionate enough to meet them. To even speak their names. Perhaps to carefully (and wisely) share with one other safe person. Maybe someone with the expertise and training to help. Because your exhausted, hard-working firefighters deserve that. They want so much to help you hurt less.

Just like with managers, there are far more firefighters than we can list here, and you won't truly know yours until you turn your attention to them and invite them to show you who they are in your system. But for now, mark the ones you may have that are bringing the most pain or negative consequences into your life. The ones that need the most healing.

- Getting Small
- Dissociating
- Overeating
- Undereating
- Alcohol Use/Addiction

- Shopping
- Fantasy
- Drug Use/Addiction
- Sexual Acting Out
- Porn
- Denial
- Numbness
- Oversleeping
- Undersleeping
- Overworking
- Underworking
- Self-Harm
- Suicidality
- Homicidality
- Violence
- Rage
- Obsession
- Compulsion
- Cutting Off
- Shutting Down
- Other:

It's hard to even think about those, I know. And yet, with these industrious firefighters, what will your next step(s) be? Be specific and concrete. Use the resources listed in the appendix, "IFS Resources," to add support to your ideas.

Now look over all three lists—exiles, managers, firefighters. Look with eyes of compassion and love.

What has made it difficult in your past to relate well to these parts?

How are you helped by knowing all parts are welcome?

What one step can you commit to take this week to relate more help-fully to one of these parts?

If you'd like to delve more deeply into how to unburden, heal, and change, you'll find options listed in the appendix, "IFS Resources," including how to find an IFS therapist near you. (There are free, down-loadable "knowing-your-parts" worksheets available on my website, also listed in the appendix.) We will never be entirely unburdened this side of heaven, but we can sure get a lot closer than most of us are right now. Take heart. You are already well on your way.

Now take several deep breaths and slowly bring your attention back to the chapter. Take a break for a moment if you need to and practice some healthy self-care. When you are ready, we'll move on to explore how parts awareness can help us in how we relate with God.

12

RELATING MORE EFFECTIVELY: ME TO GOD

Surrender, not striving

The great news is, when I'm relating with parts awareness to myself, I am much better able to access my authentic spiritual faith, my God Image. I find real and authentic relationship with God and the fruit of the Spirit flowing out of my soul.

The God Image is within us. When we grasp this reality, suddenly we can fully embrace the scriptures that teach us we have everything we need already inside of us for the life God has designed for us to live!

The task is to invite our parts to unblend enough to allow spontaneous experience of the fruit of the Spirit that already indwells us. It suddenly makes sense why it is not a matter of figuring out how to manufacture fruit; it is being present to the fruit that already is. It is surrender.

I'm reminded of the story about the great artist Michelangelo sculpting. When Michelangelo was asked what he was doing, he said he "saw the angel in the marble and carved until I set him free." Once the excess marble was invited to step back (so to speak), the beauty within was released.

Michelangelo believed he was not *creating* the angel so much as *releasing it*. So it is with our access to the Imago Dei within.

What a relief—and what a profound shift from our typical "I'm here and God's over there" theology. That kind of thinking requires us to try various techniques to get closer to where God is located so we can more fully draw on his power for living. The conundrum is perfectly captured by the saying I've often read on reader boards in front of churches: "If God feels distant, he hasn't moved. Who has?" Which we understand to mean, "Figure out how to fix yourself and get back on over there to him, where you should have been in the first place before you messed up and got over here."

I'm so glad to know that, instead of striving, we can surrender. And how do we do that? We surrender by simply conducting a Spiritual MRI (asking, "How do I feel *toward* this part, person, or experience?"). If there are parts detected, we gently ask them to step back, or unblend. With our patient attention, this practice gives us access to and releases our core self, just as Michelangelo opened up the marble and released the angel.

Going Deeper: A me-to-God exercise

Write down any situations you can remember when you have struggled to relate to God or to the church or to people of faith in the past.

Journal about why those situations have been difficult for you. What specifically has made it hard?

How have you responded to this spiritual difficulty in the past?

Has that action caused you to *feel* closer to, or further from, God? More accepted by God or less?

Now let's try a parts approach to this situation. Step back into this challenging memory, and this time do a Spiritual MRI by simply noticing how you feel *toward* God (or the church, or people of faith). You may notice feelings like: distant, angry, resentful, powerless, hopeless, exhausted, or afraid. Write down what you notice.

Next, notice if you have any feelings *about* those feelings. For example, you may feel anxious and afraid, as if God is waiting to punish you, and then you might feel shame *about* feeling anxious and afraid. (*"I shouldn't feel afraid! God is loving!"*) Write down those feelings *about* your initial feelings.

Congratulations! You have just identified a polarization inside you. IFS uses *polarization* to describe two parts in a system that orbit each other in opposition or competition. In the example above, anxiety/fear is polarized with shame/should. Both are burdened parts, at war with each other, blocking your access to the authentic God Image within you.

Draw or journal that polarization.

Take a moment to bring some curiosity to each part that you're aware of.

Part 1 (for example, anxious/afraid that God will punish): What do you notice about it? When did it first begin to feel this way? What does it need from you?

Part 2 (for example, shame/should about feeling anxious/afraid): What do you notice about it? How is it trying to help you? What is it afraid would happen if it didn't fight against Part 1?

Once you understand each of these parts better, invite them both to step back and give you access to your God Image within. If one or both are unwilling to step back, ask what they are afraid would happen if they did step back. Reassure each of them that you will not allow the other part to take over, and see if they would be willing to each step back the same amount. If they do step back, you will notice an opening of spaciousness in your body, and a sense of the Eight Cs / fruit of the Spirit. You've connected with God In Here. Journal about what that is like for you.

As you have seen, it is surrender (parts stepping back) rather than striving (trying harder) that accesses God In Here. How does experiencing this reality change things for you? What surprises you about this? What feels right to you about it?

What is one time this week you might set aside to continue to invite your parts to unblend and experience God In Here? Use the "Going Deeper: Accessing your God Image" exercise (chapter 3, p. 36) if that's helpful to get you started.

Take several deep breaths and slowly bring your attention back to the chapter. If you like, take a break for some healthy self-care before we go on. The next chapter is longer and includes several "Going Deeper" exercises. That's because now that we've explored relating more effectively within ourselves and with God, it's time to turn our attention to a broader demographic: how we relate with other people. Whenever you're ready.

13

RELATING MORE EFFECTIVELY: ME TO OTHERS

Four ways to use what we've learned

One important benefit of parts awareness is that it allows us to relate to other people in our lives in a much more compassionate and effective way. Over the course of the previous chapters, we've set out key principles that reorient our relationships entirely. In this chapter, we'll get specific about four ways we put those principles into practice.

1. Move Toward, Not Against or Away

Remember, it has been a battle since the beginning of the church to move toward and not against. Or away. So, it makes sense that we need some parts awareness before we can do this with ease.

As we've seen, the Pharisees—as well-intentioned as they might have been—were big on moving against and away. They demanded that people follow enormously complex rules to ensure they were pure enough to come near the temple. In effect, they scorned those who were in touch with their exiles.

Luke 18:10–12 paints the picture clearly: "Two men went up to the temple to pray, one a Pharisee and the other a tax collector. The Pharisee stood by himself and prayed: 'God, I thank you that I am not like other people—robbers, evildoers, adulterers—or even like this tax collector. I fast twice a week and give a tenth of all I get.'" That's a pretty clear picture of *move away*.

Going Deeper: Moving toward and moving away

Have you ever experienced a move away coming from someone representing God? What was that experience like for you?

If you were aware of a vulnerable part of you that was feeling judged or rejected by a move-away experience, what did that part of you need most in that moment?

What would it have looked like for someone instead to move toward you then?

Pharisees were all about doing the right things out of their hard-working manager parts, but were moving strongly against their own exiles/firefighters and away from the exiles/firefighters of others. As a result, they probably missed the encounter with God they already had within them. And definitely missed the encounter with God that Jesus offered outside of them.

The church had a slightly different take on this in the days of Martin Luther, demanding certain payments and behaviors (managers doing the right things to get them close to God), but institutionally missing the experience of God within. At varying times in history, burdened parts within the church have sanctioned the Crusades, slavery, apartheid, injustice toward native peoples, colonialism, Jim Crow laws, the Holocaust, and other violence against humans.

I'm pretty sure Jesus would have called all that being "whitewashed tombs."[58] I think that translates to, "Your managers aren't helping here."

This sends chills through my bones. Consistently throughout church history, we have missed the move-toward possibilities and started believing that moving against and away was the heart of God. So often, our most sincere efforts to get close to God appear to have taken us further from him.

I can think of many times that my own well-meaning parts have done church in move-against ways. Can you?

Take a moment, with compassion, to record some of yours here. What did some of your specific move-against moments look like?

It may be hard to read that list now, but can you compassionately identify the experience or feeling the move-against part of you was trying to help you avoid?

In just one of those circumstances, what would a move-toward approach have looked and felt like?

What would it have required you to risk?

Doing church from burdened managers and not from our God Image unfortunately hurts us and hurts other people. It drives us further from God and breaks our relationship with him, with each other, and with ourselves.

If you, like me, have ever lived in a posture of moving against any of our parts or the parts of others, what a relief to know that we can accept this powerful invitation to move toward. To decline to participate any longer in whitewashed-tomb churching or living.

When we move toward others we recognize that they have God's very likeness imprinted on their core, and that any wonky thing they may be doing is because they have a part stuck in a bad role. We can view that part with compassion and curiosity rather than resentment or fear, because we understand it is just trying to help.

When we move toward with that curiosity and compassion, we are in our God Image. Witnessing. Loving. Comforting. If they are unwell or unsafe, we can also set effective boundaries for our safety or wellness from our God Image. Without agenda or pressure or threats or shame. Just love.

That's my God. Doing what he does best. Love.

That was the essence of the gospel, wasn't it? Something about "the greatest commandment is to love." The whole big, honking, heavy Bible condensed down into one word: *love*.

2. Make a U-Turn

One of IFS's more transformational takeaways for me has been that when we understand parts—ours and others—we develop something like superpowers for relating more successfully to people. All people. Especially those that make us crazy.

The IFS concept of the U-turn proposes that, when a situation or person is triggering for us, rather than looking at what they are doing wrong, we turn our attention around and notice the parts of us that are getting activated. Rather than exclaiming, "That person is driving me crazy!" we ask, "What is coming up in me?"

With this simple redirect, the difficult people in our lives suddenly become gifts, serving as our tor-mentors. (We touched on this dynamic in chapter 8.)

By tormenting us with those frustrating and annoying things they do, they serve as mentors for the parts of us that need healing.

Yeah. Okay. What exactly does that look like?

How about an example that's entirely fabricated? Or not. (I'll let you decide.)

Let's say Denise has an exile that is very, very uncomfortable with being loud or noticed in public. At all. She shrinks in terror from the thought. For whatever reason, she feels fear when attention is drawn to her in public spaces, and she has a firefighter that works overtime to help her be small, quiet, and demur in just those contexts. Her husband, on the other hand, is a large and loud man. At six foot four, he is noticeable in any setting. Did I mention he is deaf in one ear? So, his already resonant basso profundo voice naturally amps up because he doesn't know he's being loud.

There you have their chronic marital conflict in a nutshell. They've fought about volume for years. It's kind of funny. Except for her it's so not.

But if instead of getting frustrated, Denise takes the invitation to view her husband as her tor-mentor, she can take a U-turn when he starts speaking loudly. Rather than focusing on him and all the things he is doing wrong (being loud, drawing attention), she can turn her attention back to herself—to her parts that are getting activated. The gift her beloved offers is the activation of her parts that need to be healed. She asks herself the driving U-Turn question: "What feelings are coming up in me right now?" and she immediately connects with the parts of her that are overly worried about judgment and criticism.

When she notices those parts and their need for healing, she has the option to give them access to her God Image, to be witnessed, and to be unburdened. So that she no longer cringes at matters of volume. And can be present with her loud and wonderful beloved.

The U-Turn question is, "What feelings are coming up in me right now?"

In the book of Matthew, Jesus put it this way: "Why do you look at the speck of sawdust in your brother's eye and pay no attention to the plank in your own eye? How can you say to your brother, 'Let me take the speck out of your eye,' when all the time there is a plank in your own eye?"[59]

Going Deeper: Taking a U-turn

Now how about you? Who is that person in your life that drives you bananas? It may be a politician, a neighbor, a boss, or a friend.

What do they do that makes you so upset?

How do you usually respond?

Does that change them in any way? Does it help the situation?

Now, instead of focusing on what they are doing wrong, redirect your attention toward yourself. What feelings, thoughts, or beliefs are getting activated in you?

Can you ask this part or these parts of you what they need? Perhaps your tor-mentor is repeatedly abusive and instead of staying frozen, your parts need to follow through with a boundary. Perhaps you have a critical part that needs unburdening. Just be curious and write down what you notice.

Wonderful! You have just identified what IFS calls a *trailhead*—an entry point in you to an area that needs healing. Notice how much more effective it is to direct our awareness to ourselves (which we can do something about) rather than focusing on someone or something else (over which we are powerless).

The U-turn can seriously transform our whole lives. All we have to do is ask, "What feelings are coming up in me?" With that inward look, we become better able to respond positively to difficult people.

3. Speak *For*, Not *From*

When our parts are blended and have taken over, we feel like we *are* the part. When our Angry part is up front, we feel angry, act angry, and speak angrily. We often think we *are* an angry person. The same goes for Sadness, Anxiety, Control, or any other part.

When the part is in control, we have to speak *from* it. We speak as though we *are* it. Of course, as with all things parts driven, when we speak *from* a part, we rarely accomplish what we desire.

When we are angry, for example, we usually want our pain seen and honored, and we want someone to make amends for the wrong they've done to us. The unfortunate thing is, if we are screaming at someone in rage, they are unlikely to see our pain; they are likely to develop their own pain and their own defended parts to protect them from our rage. All of which moves us further away from our goal of being seen and honored.

Hmm.

With a parts awareness, we have the ability to invite the Angry part to unblend and separate from us, and now we have the capacity to speak *for* it. This makes all the difference.

If an Angry part is activated in me because I've had a boundary violated, being able to find my inner God Image as separate from the Angry part allows me to understand why I'm angry, to acknowledge the pain and hurt of the exiles behind the anger, and to speak that pain, hurt, and anger in a healthy way.

To speak *for* a part, we simply have to:

1. Realize a part is present. (That's anytime we are feeling something other than the Eight Cs.)
2. Invite the part to unblend so we have God Image access.
3. Invite the part to share what it feels and needs.
4. Acknowledge the part's concerns and make sure we've understood correctly.
5. Ask permission to speak for—that means *on behalf of*—the part.

This process creates a shift in our energy. Body language, tone of voice, emotions, and facial expression all shift when parts unblend and we access our God Image. From this powerful core, we can speak for our parts and have a far greater chance of being heard.

When we speak for our parts, we typically say things like, "a part of me feels _____ and another part of me feels _____." This simple tool then allows us to give voice to parts of us that may even hold conflicting opinions: "A part of me feels furious that you didn't pick up Samantha from school today, and another part of me feels aware and understanding that you had that important meeting with your boss and lost track of time." We have a much better chance of being truly and nondefensively heard, and our parts also calm down because they feel well represented.

Let's return to Jane from chapter 8 and her betrayal trauma from discovering her husband, John, was addicted to porn and having affairs. She may be rightfully feeling anger, sorrow, and rejection (among many other things). If she speaks *from* her parts, she might say something like this:

What the h—is wrong with you? How could you do this to us? You son of a #$@! I never should have married you in the first place. George wanted to marry me, and he was a much better man than you. I should have married him. He never would have done this to his family. Get out, you filthy adulterer! You sicken me!

Now, you and I both know what she really wants is for John to see the depths of the pain his actions have caused her, to tell her that her feelings are completely valid, and that he deserves to hear how deeply she is wounded. She wants her husband to move toward her with deep remorse, regret, and brokenness. To assure her that she is his dearest love and that he was an idiot for betraying her. To tell her that he will do anything in the world to win her back, no matter how long it takes.

Right? Yep. For 99 percent of the betrayed spouses I work with, that's what they want.

Notice however, that when Jane speaks *from* her anger and hurt, John is very likely to feel attacked, shamed, and unwanted. His defensive parts—rage, blame shifting, shutdown, withdrawing—are likely to go up.

When she says those things, he is unlikely to be able to stay with his God Image and truly hear her pain and honor it. Instead, things are likely to dissolve into a shouting match or a silent war where both people feel unloved, unseen, uncared for, and abandoned.

Now, John's actions have caused this problem for sure, and it is his responsibility to work on staying in his God Image to be able to honor the pain he has caused.

Absolutely.

However, Jane's need to have her pain seen and honored recedes in intensity when she speaks *for* her pain and hurt rather than *from* it.

Notice how she might speak *for* those same hurt and angry parts:

> *John, I need to let you know that parts of me feel hurt, rejected, angry, betrayed, alone, and afraid about your porn use and affairs, because I have built my life and our marriage around the belief that we would be faithful to each other. And this causes me profoundly deep pain as I grieve that loss. Would you be willing to listen to my pain, seek counseling, and cut off the relationship with your affair partner? If you choose to, I will consider being able to remain in this relationship. If you choose not to, I will need to separate myself in order to honor my pain and my integrity.*

Speaking for our parts honors our pain, underscores our integrity, honors the recipient of our words, and gives us the greatest likelihood of being heard.

Now it's your turn.

Going Deeper: Speaking from and speaking for

When was the last time you remember speaking *from* a part?

Which part of you was it?

What did you say?

How did it go? Did you feel heard, cared for, and successful in your communication?

Now imagine how you might instead have spoken *for* that part or those parts of you. Write out what you might have said.

"A part of me feels . . . "

"And another part of me feels . . . "

(Perhaps) "And another part of me feels . . . "

How do you imagine that might have gone?

How might you have felt inside? Would this have represented your parts more effectively?

It's simple but not at all easy. As we put this wisdom into practice, we'll see immediate, even radical changes in how we relate in emotionally fraught situations.

4. A Part Is Not the Whole

I love this truth, because it frees me to be multidimensional, meaning I have more freedom and flexibility in the way I relate to others.

When the guy on I-285 suddenly veers in front of me at a high rate of speed and then flips *me* off, I can know that an angry *part* of him is up front at the moment, but that is not who he is. And if he has an angry part that is stuck in some extreme behavior—like cutting in and flipping me off—there's something driving that for him. He probably has some exiles that believe their feelings and needs don't matter, and they probably are pretty raw because his angry part seems reactive and aggressive, trying to—in unhelpful ways—take care of his feelings and needs.

Does that make his actions on the freeway okay?

Absolutely not. But a multidimensional perspective can help me stay in my God Image (or at least closer to it) and not react by allowing *my* angry part to take over because I feel like my feelings and needs don't matter. That perspective also allows some space between people's actions and who they are. Space for me to breathe. And remain calm.

Let's bring this closer to home. If you are married, your spouse has some behaviors that drive you crazy or make you angry. If you are single, someone close to you does things that make you bananas. That's the nature of living in community with imperfect people.

Going Deeper: A part is not the whole

Think of that irritating thing your person does. Really think about it for a moment. And notice when you think unidimensionally—*He/she is such a jerk!*—what feelings and thoughts come up for you. Write them down.

You may notice that various parts of you get activated and take over. Perhaps an angry, resentful, or withdrawn part. Perhaps a part that thinks, *This is the wrong person for me. I should not be in relationship with them.* Because, honestly, when they are doing that jerky thing they do, if that was all of who they were, you might actually not want to be in relationship with them.

Now take a breath and think of this behavior as just a part of them. Can you identify it as a manager or a firefighter?

What exile(s) might it be protecting?

Do you know anything about where that potential exile may have developed?

Remind yourself that is not who they are; it is just a part of them. Now, notice how you feel. Notice any shifts in your internal experience. Record those here:

You might notice that you feel calmer. More rational. More able to cope wisely with their jerky behavior. And more able to hold on to the love or care you authentically do feel for them.

Hear me say this again: *This does not make their bad behavior okay.*

If their behavior is dangerous or repeatedly dishonoring—if they are physically, verbally, or sexually abusive and endangering, or continually lie and betray with no remorse or consistent attempts to change—then you can stay in God Image, set healthy boundaries, and possibly move away from the relationship to keep yourself emotionally, physically, financially, or sexually safe. In fact, when we are in our God Image, we are much more able to wisely observe whether healthy boundaries are being respected—remembering that a healthy boundary is about keeping oneself safe and not about changing someone else's behavior. We are more able also to actually follow through, because our wounded, fearful parts are not running the show.

Knowing that a part is not the whole is also freeing as I relate to myself.

When I honor my multidimensionality, I am freed to acknowledge and honor all the parts of me, not just picking one as my identity. I get space to breathe as I relate to my God-given complexity. Just acknowledging that a particular part is not *me* but is *a part of me that is trying to help* goes a long way toward giving me better strategies for interacting with it.

How about you? Do you have a part that you regularly overidentify with? Perhaps you tell yourself, "I'm such a bad mom" or "I'm a loner" or "I'm such a messed-up person." Write down the negative messages you send yourself.

Now recognize that is *just one part* of you that holds that belief or those feelings or actions. It is not *who you are*. How does it feel to become aware of that larger reality?

Do you feel the access that you have to a wider array of behaviors and feelings and choices?

What is that shift like for you?

As we reach the end of this chapter, take a moment to reflect on your most challenging relationships. Which one of the principles we've discussed would give you more freedom and flexibility as you relate to that person or those people?

1) Move toward, not against or away
2) Make a U-turn
3) Speak for, not from
4) A part is not the whole

Which of these four concepts will be easiest for you to implement?

What makes it the easiest?

What would shift in your life if you became more intentional about applying these principles?

Now take several deep breaths and slowly bring your attention back to the chapter. Take a break if you like and practice some healthy self-care. Maybe meditate. Drink a cup of tea. Go for a brisk walk. Call a supportive friend. Take a nap. Whatever it looks like for you, take good care of your parts.

As we wrap up our exploration of how to apply parts awareness in our everyday lives, we have one more dynamic to consider: group to group and culture to culture. When you're ready, I'll meet you there.

14

RELATING MORE EFFECTIVELY: GROUP TO GROUP AND CULTURE TO CULTURE

Parts awareness and polarized communities

The amazing thing about parts awareness is that it applies not only to our relationships with ourselves, God, and others, but also to our larger communities and cultures. When we see the divisions in our global landscape as burdened exiles and protectors, we begin to make sense of the increasingly polarized communities in which we find ourselves and discover hope that things might actually change.

In a very real sense, we have burdened parts at war in our global sociopolitical economy. Let's consider for a moment, how there are distinct "parts" of our culture: political, educational, racial, religious, sexual, and the list could go on. When we have pain in the history of our culture (and of course we do), cultural exiles will develop who carry the burdens of that pain. In response, burdened managers and firefighters will emerge to try to keep their pain at bay within the social system at large.

Who are the exiles of our communities? Well, just as in our inner worlds, these are groups within our culture who have experienced powerlessness and hurt in some way. This could include people of color, women, children, the poor, the uneducated, those who struggle with mental health, and immigrant groups. This would also include groups who are overtly abused by larger cultural forces such as victims of human trafficking. Just like our inner exiles, these groups are burdened by the pain of their injuries. And just like in our inner systems, suppressing or avoiding that pain will be a driving energy in the larger system until it is witnessed, validated, and unburdened. In a very real sense, as long as the harm done to disempowered parts of our society goes unresolved, burdened cultural protectors will have to become more and more extreme as our global system attempts to avoid, deny, or suppress the cultural exile pain.

The increasing polarization of, for example, our political system makes enormous sense in light of these dynamics. Burdened managers and firefighters will necessarily emerge in our societies, and they will employ the same tactics as the managers and firefighters in our inner worlds: blame, shame, deny, minimize, etc. They may be abusive, overindulgent, or attacking. Focus will be given to further exiling the exiles, because just as in our inner worlds, protectors are afraid of the exiles' pain and want to "kick them out" of the system or "make them go away." The more intense the exile pain, the more intense the tactics of the protectors. So, the ends of our political spectrum will become more and more extreme, while the more moderate contingent becomes "unelectable."

Remember, this is not because any party or person or philosophy is fundamentally good or bad; it is simply the natural result of increasing, unresolved pain in our global system. Burdened protectors activate when burdened exiles are carrying unresolved hurt. When we have catastrophic cultural pain, such as mass shootings, terrorism, pandemics, and global warming, large sections of our culture (if not the entire culture) become further burdened with exile pain, even if they don't happen to hold minority or disempowered status. We develop global exiles.

When burdened protectors drive our dialogue and worldviews, we resonate with anger, hatred, hopelessness, and an us-versus-them mentality. We each will bring our own discernment to identify how much this may be the case in our individual experience. We can do a cultural MRI just as easily as a spiritual one by asking ourselves, "How do I feel *toward* #metoo, immigration policy, abortion, welfare reform, tax policy, Republicans, Independents, Democrats, Socialists . . . ?" If the answer is anything other than the Eight Cs, we are not in our cultural Imago Dei. Not in our helpful core, from which we see the God Image clearly in those who hold opinions different from ours, whose family structure, education, cultural background, or immigrant status does not reflect our own.

Precious few individuals have ever brought their core selves to this more global stage. In order to do so, we must be deeply led by the God Image within our own individual systems. You know immediately who they are. They changed the world as they brought the qualities of the God Image to the global stage.

Jesus
Martin Luther King, Jr.
Mahatma Gandhi
Nelson Mandela
Mother Teresa

What comes to mind when you think of their character? Of their impact on the world? What qualities? Chances are good that you think of love, compassion, nonviolence, grace toward enemies, humility, and the ability to influence the trajectory of world events.

And so it is true.

Love does win.

Love is the defining characteristic of our God Image. The defining quality of our God. The single commandment Jesus left for us. The value Paul called "the greatest of these."[60] The first fruit of the Spirit. As simplistic as this may seem, it is profoundly transformative, whether it is directed inward toward our own hurting parts or outward toward the parts of others. We do not overcome burdens with more burdens. We transform burdens with love. With the loving, compassionate presence of our Imago Dei core.

Love does win.

Love overflowing from our core divine within can and does change the course of history. When we read the headlines or are overwhelmed with the suffering of our neighbor or friend, we can definitively, concretely, tangibly change the course of the human events in our sphere of influence by bringing enough love to our own parts that we can then hold love for the parts of all others. When we think of the political group, the ethnic group, the economic group that activates us the most, we can take a U-turn, bring compassionate curiosity to our own burdens that activate, and then in turn bring our healing core spirit to that group, that person, that cause.

Imagine what a difference we could effect in our culture if we brought this God Image to our lives. If we brought Imago Dei first to ourselves, and then to our PTA meetings. Our offices. Our neighborhoods. Our policy debates. Our media coverage. Our Thanksgiving tables. Imagine what it would be like to lovingly and thoughtfully disagree. To hold openheartedness and genuine curiosity for someone on the other side of the debate or the argument. Envision with me how this alone might bring healing and compassion and connection to even the most fractious among us.

I invite you to practice *moving toward* in your daily exchanges with groups unlike your own. Be mindful of your movement in any group with which you are associated. Where do you chafe? Where do you flare? Where do you withdraw? How might you move toward instead?

We have power to enact real change. And it starts with surrender to the God In Here, bringing love inside of us so that we can bring it to all that is outside. Don't you want to be a part of that kind of world?

Going Deeper: A group-to-group exercise

It's especially in the most difficult places in life where God's image in our innermost brings hope for something different.

Where do you feel most hopeless about parts at war in our culture?

What one idea from this chapter could bring hope to that situation?

What strikes you about the simplicity of the concept Love Wins?

In what ways does that resonate with your experience?

Now, think for a moment of the political party with which you *least* identify.

Think of a leader within that party who most personifies all that you oppose. Describe them here:

Let's use the principle of a U-Turn to help us know how to better respond. What is coming up in you?

What feelings are you aware of?

- Disgust
- Anger
- Horror
- Shame
- Judgment
- Numbness
- Fear
- Anxiety
- Other:

What thoughts come to mind about this person? This party?

What sensations do you notice in your body?

- Tension in shoulders or neck
- Sick stomach
- Tingling
- Jitters
- Agitation
- Tight jaw
- Furrowed brow
- Other:

Notice how you would typically respond when this person comes to mind or comes up in discussion. How do you normally speak? Feel? Behave?

Take a moment to sit with anything that you notice. Welcome it. It probably won't feel good. That's okay. Journal anything you're aware of.

When you've had a chance to sit with each thought, feeling, and sensation, and they've hopefully had a chance to settle a bit, pick one and see if you can get to know it a little better.

Notice where you feel it in your body:

See if it will unblend from you so you can be with it.

How do you feel *toward* it? Unblend any additional parts until you feel the Eight Cs.

What does this part of you want you to know?

What is it afraid would happen if it didn't take you over?

Where did it learn to show up for you in this way?

Now, as you stay in your God Image (you will feel the Eight Cs), turn your attention toward the person you brought to mind. How do you experience them now? (If you lost the Eight Cs when they came to mind, ask your parts to let you just be with the person's image for a moment.)

Are you aware of any new thoughts or feelings about them?

Can you hold open the possibility that there might be a reason they act or speak the way they do?

What would it look like if you moved toward this person's perspective with curiosity, without giving up your felt truth? If you, in your God Image, held openness and curiosity and compassion for this person?

What parts of you resist moving toward this person? What are they afraid might happen if you did?

Journal anything that you noticed here. Notice what it was like for you to imagine this experience, and if you noticed any shifts.

Now take several deep breaths and slowly bring your attention back to the chapter. Take a break if you need to and practice some healthy self-care. This is hard stuff we are considering. Take good care of your parts.

15

FINAL THOUGHTS

Where to go from here

I hope you've experienced throughout your time in this book how parts awareness helps you to get to know your parts in an open and non-shaming way. Helps you move toward all the parts of you with openness and compassion. Helps you access your God Image, which has the power to unburden/heal your burdened parts and free them to do something more helpful for you.

It's good stuff. It really is. And oh-so-different than how we normally live. My sincere desire for you is that you will love this idea of compassion for parts as much as I do. That you will jump in with both feet and embrace this affirming, godly, gracious way of living with yourself and toward others.

To continue to develop this new relationship with your parts, I encourage you to return to the "Going Deeper" exercises throughout the book. Your parts deserve it. They deserve you! And to support you on your journey, the resources section at the back of this book (in the appendix) offers several suggestions for further exploration.

Most people find it helpful to have a trained and experienced guide in the process of personal growth. This is especially true if you have a significant history of trauma, any mental health diagnosis, or challenges with daily functioning. If this is the case for you, or if you'd prefer someone to lead you through the process, I invite you to seek out an IFS-trained therapist and truly do what's called insight work: learning how to invite parts to unblend, experiencing the healing and unburdening of exiles, and witnessing their life-changing transformation.

Without a doubt, the world would be a better place if we were all led by our God Image. I'm actually fairly persuaded this is exactly what heaven will be like. No sin (burdened parts), just our God-created being in communion with God and with each other.

So, with great honor to you and the desire to live with integrity to the themes of this book, I offer you my gratitude for coming on this journey. For considering a new lens through which to view yourself and the world around you. For bringing the compassionate God Image in you to a conversation about faith, life, and love.

Discussion Questions

- What is your biggest takeaway from this book?
- What one next step would you like to take toward living a God Image life?

GLOSSARY OF TERMS

activated: When a part feels threatened (either by experiencing something that reminds it of a past hurt, or by the activity of a polarized part) and begins to flood, or take over, an individual's internal system.

blend or **blending:** Blending happens when a part takes over and completely obscures access to the core self, or God Image. When a part blends, the individual feels its feelings, thinks its thoughts, and experiences its physical sensations. It feels as though the person *is* the part. *Blend* is the opposite of terms like *step back*, *unblend*, *separate*, or *relax*. (Synonyms: *flood, take over*.)

burdens: Extreme feelings, beliefs, or behaviors that attach to parts as a result of negative life experiences. A burden is like a shackled weight that attaches to a part (thus, transforming it into an exile or a protector), causing the part to lose access to its naturally created positive essence.

Eight C qualities of Self:

- *calmness*: Physiological and emotional serenity regardless of circumstances; ability to respond to triggers in nonextreme ways; ability to avoid fight-flight-freeze responses when threatened.

- *clarity*: The ability to perceive situations accurately without distortions from extreme beliefs and emotions; the ability to maintain objectivity; the absence of preconception.

- *curiosity*: Strong desire to learn something new; a sense of wonder and awe; genuine interest in nonjudgmental understanding.

- *compassion*: Openhearted presence and empathy for another without the desire to fix or control; a sense of connection with the suffering of others.

- *confidence*: Strong belief in one's ability.

- *courage*: Strength in the face of threat, challenge, or danger; willingness to take action toward a large or overwhelming goal.

- *creativity*: Ability to create generative learning, solutions, and expressions of original ideas; spontaneous flow of expression and immersion into the pleasure of an activity.

- *connectedness*: Quality of being connected to a larger community; spiritual connection to a meaningful purpose and higher calling in life; presence of relaxed relationship free from the interference of burdened parts and fear of judgment.

exile: A part that has become burdened by negative life experiences and has therefore lost access to its naturally positive qualities. Exiles carry negative emotions like fear, shame, loneliness, anxiety, and sadness, as well as negative beliefs such as "I'm all alone," "My feelings and needs don't matter," and "Something is wrong with me."

firefighter: A burdened protector part that attempts to extinguish the pain of exile(s) reactively, after the exile has been triggered. Common firefighter strategies include addictions, disordered eating, self-harm, violence, dissociation, obsession, compulsion, fantasy, rage.

flood or **flooding:** Flooding happens when a part takes over and completely obscures access to the core self, or God Image. When a part floods, the individual feels its feelings, thinks its thoughts, and experiences its physical sensations. It feels as though the person *is* the part. Flood is the opposite of terms like *step back*, *unblend*, *separate*, or *relax*. (Synonyms: *take over*, *blend*.)

Internal Family Systems (IFS): A model of therapy developed by Dr. Richard Schwartz that understands human beings to be comprised of a core Self (referred to in this book as *God Image* or *Imago Dei*) and many different parts.

manager: A burdened protector part that attempts to manage or control events proactively, to prevent the pain of exile(s) from being activated. Common manager strategies include controlling, people pleasing, striving, judging, self-criticizing, and attempting to do things perfectly.

parts: Unique aspects of our personalities (subpersonalities) that have their own thoughts, feelings, sensations, and agendas. All people are born with many unburdened parts that together comprise their unique personality. All parts want something positive for the individual. Some parts become burdened with pain (or strategies for coping with pain) from negative life experiences.

polarized: When two parts in a system are working in opposition to each other. Managers and firefighters are often polarized. Each part strives to counteract the behavior of the other part.

protectors: Parts in a system that have become burdened with extreme roles in an attempt to eliminate exile pain. There are two types of protectors: managers, that try to proactively prevent exile pain from becoming activated, and firefighters, that try to reactively extinguish exile pain once it has been triggered.

Self (God Image or *Imago Dei*): Our central core that is who we truly are. The Self is the seat of our authentic spiritual connection to the divine. In this book, we primarily use the term *God Image*, or *Imago Dei*, to refer to Self, which reflects the Christian understanding that humans are made in the image of God (Genesis 1:27). The God Image is undamaged in all people and reflects qualities of the divine such as the fruit of the Spirit or the Eight C qualities. The goal of IFS therapy, and of Christian living, is to lead our internal parts from this core.

Six Fs for getting to know a part: (1) Find, (2) Focus, (3) Flesh Out, (4) Feel, (5) BeFriend, and (6) Fear.

Spiritual MRI: Noticing how one feels *toward* a part, person, or experience. Any feelings that do not reflect the Eight Cs indicate there is a part blended and the individual does not have access to their core God Image.

tor-mentor: An IFS term for an activating situation or person. By noticing what parts become active in oneself in response to a tor-mentor, an individual will be able to identify their own burdened parts that need healing. Thus, "tormenting" people and situations are a great gift to one's own personal growth and healing.

unblend: The process whereby a blended part feels safe enough, or relaxed enough, to release control and step back from the central experience of the individual. When a part unblends, the person will notice an abating of its emotions, sensations, and thoughts from their immediate awareness. (Synonyms: *step back, separate, relax*.)

IFS RESOURCES

BOOKS AND WORKBOOKS

Cook, Alison and Kimberly Miller. *Boundaries for Your Soul: How to Turn Your Overwhelming Thoughts and Feelings into Your Greatest Allies.* Nashville, TN: Nelson Books, 2018.

Earley, Jay. *Self-Therapy: A Step-By-Step Guide to Creating Wholeness and Healing Your Inner Child Using IFS, a New, Cutting-Edge Psychotherapy.* Larkspur, CA: Pattern System Books, 2010.

Holmes, Tom. *Parts Work: An Illustrated Guide to Your Inner Life.* Kalamazoo, MI: Winged Heart Press, 2007.

Scazzero, Peter. *Emotionally Healthy Spirituality: It's Impossible to be Spiritually Mature, While Remaining Emotionally Immature.* Grand Rapids, MI: Zondervan, 2006.

Schwartz, Richard C. *Internal Family Systems Therapy.* New York: Guilford, 1995.

———. *Introduction to the Internal Family Systems Model.* Oak Park, IL: Trailheads Publications, 2001.

———. *You Are the One You've Been Waiting For: Bringing Courageous Love to Intimate Relationships.* Oak Park, IL: Trailheads Publishing, 2008.

Weiss, Bonnie J. *Self-Therapy Workbook: An Exercise Book for the IFS Process.* Larkspur, CA: Pattern System Books, 2014.

WEBSITES

Author's Website:

www.jennariemersma.com

Additional resources available on the author's website include IFS videos as well as free, downloadable worksheets for individual parts work.

IFS Institute Website:

https://ifs-institute.com/

Although web addresses for detailed resources shift from time to time, the following URLs for specific pages on the IFS Institute website were accurate at the time of publication.

IFS Therapist Locator

A comprehensive listing of therapists who have completed at least Level 1 training in Internal Family Systems Therapy is available at this link:

https://ifs-institute.com/practitioners

Clinicians listed as "Certified IFS Therapists" have completed all three levels of Internal Family Systems Therapy training and maintain ongoing continuing education in IFS work.

IFS Therapeutic Retreats:

https://ifs-institute.com/news-events/retreats

IFS Workshops:

https://ifs-institute.com/news-events/workshops

IFS Online Learning Opportunities:

https://ifs-institute.com/online-learning

NOTES

1. See Exodus 22:25–27.
2. See the story of Jacob wrestling with God in Genesis 32:22–32.
3. Acts 13:22.
4. Frank Newport, "Church Leaders and Declining Religious Service Attendance," Gallup website (September 7, 2018), accessed January 10, 2019. https://news.gallup.com /opinion/polling-matters/242015/church-leaders-declining-religious-service-attendance .aspx?.
5. See John 16:33.
6. Richard Schwartz, *Introduction to the Internal Family Systems Model* (Oak Park, IL: Trailheads Publications, 2001), 17.
7. When I refer to our core self, I most often use the term *God Image* to avoid confusion for Christians who understand the fallen or fleshly self to be deeply flawed. In this book, references to *Self* without other faith-informed modifiers (e.g., God Image, Spirit Self, created Self) should be understood as the Self as described by Dr. Richard Schwartz in *Internal Family Systems Therapy*.
8. Schwartz, *Introduction*, 18.
9. First Corinthians 12:12, 18–21, 26–27 (emphasis mine).
10. Schwartz, *Introduction*, 19.
11. John Lynch, *TrueFaced: Trust God and Others with Who You Really Are* (Colorado Springs, CO: Navpress, 2004).
12. Romans 7:15.
13. First John 4:18.
14. See 1 John 4, especially verses 8 and 16.
15. Genesis 1:31.
16. Genesis 3:7.
17. Genesis 3:7.
18. Genesis 3:8.
19. Genesis 3:9–10.
20. Genesis 3:11.
21. Genesis 3:12.
22. Genesis 3:13.
23. Colossians 1:27.
24. See Hebrews 13:5; Deuteronomy 31:8; Joshua 1:9; 1 Chronicles 28:20; Isaiah 41:10.

25. See Colossians 1:27.

26. Romans 8:38–39.

27. Galatians 5:22–23 (ESV).

28. Schwartz, *Introduction*, 49–50.

29. Mark 1:41.

30. Therapists encourage clients to give voice to their pain—often a real challenge for people who grew up in unhealthy families with unspoken rules like "Don't talk." That kind of silence-keeping translates to a learned inability to name for ourselves and others what's really going on, and how we really feel.

31. Matthew 19:14.

32. First Peter 5:7.

33. John 11:33–34.

34. John 11:35.

35. See the appendix, "IFS Resources."

36. Luke 10:41.

37. Galatians 6:5.

38. Melissa Haas, *A L.I.F.E Recovery Guide for Spouses,* (Lake Mary, FL: Freedom Everyday, 2008).

39. Mark 12:30–31.

40. John 15:12.

41. John 15:17.

42. Matthew 23:27–28.

43. John 13:35.

44. Richard Schwartz.

45. James 4:1.

46. John 8:7.

47. See Matthew 5:39.

48. See Matthew 18:22.

49. See Matthew 27:46.

50. Philippians 4:8, emphasis mine.

51. Joshua 1:8, emphasis mine.

52. Psalm 1:1–2, emphasis mine.

53. Genesis 3:22.

54. Mark 15:34.

55. Ephesians 2:8–9.

56. Galatians 5:19–21a.

57. See John 8:1–11.

58. Matthew 23:27.

59. Matthew 7:3–4.

60. First Corinthians 13:13.

ACKNOWLEDGEMENTS

Writing a book is truly a labor of love, and one which I could not have undertaken without a vast community of support. I honor and extend my heartfelt gratitude to all who have lent their encouragement and expertise to the creation of this book. To the incredible team of skilled professionals who guided me expertly through every step of this process and cared for its message with as much love and honor as if it was your own, thank you. Words are not adequate to express my appreciation, although I will offer my feeble attempt here.

To David Kopp, my editor and friend, I am forever indebted. Your faithful encouragement, brilliant editorial skills, and gracious heart helped to make this book what it is. Your ability to finesse complex content into something readable is nothing short of amazing, and your good-humored patience with my novice's understanding of book making has blessed me more than you will ever know. To Heather Kopp, skilled collaborator and friend, for your insightful titling skills, your supportive input and expert guidance, I am also deeply grateful. The support, faith, courage, and generosity you have both brought to me and to this message are gifts that I will always treasure.

To Dr. Alexia Rothman, so much of this book is because of you. From your first IFS workshop to the hours of supervision and mentoring you have shared, your Self-led, kind, and gracious presence has poured deeply into my heart and I am filled with appreciation. You never stopped believing in me and the message of this book, and it has come into reality in large part because of you. With all my heart I thank you.

Randy, you are the most supportive and encouraging husband I could possibly ask for. Thank you for being my biggest fan, for encouraging me on the hard days, cheering me on the good days, and cooking for me on all the days. Thank you for your patience with long hours of writing and your never-ending belief in me. I love you.

To my two amazing children, Rebecca and Steven, you are two of the biggest blessings in my life. You inspire me with your lives and with your hearts. I love you dearly and I like you deeply. I couldn't be a prouder mom.

To Wendy, I could not ask for a more skillful assistant, a more capable advocate, or a better friend. You fix my microphones, find my Power-Points, and make late-night runs to Walmart for hairspray. How did I ever manage without you? God knew that I needed you.

To Dick Schwartz, I owe a debt of gratitude for your lifetime of dedication to bringing the important message of IFS to the world. Thank you for believing in me, for supporting this book, and for bringing your wise and caring Self to the world. I am forever changed because of you!

To my dear friends and colleagues Elizabeth Moore, Sandy Flesner, Nancy Chiles, Dr. Christine Baker, Amanda Bird, Marnie Ferree, Laura Casper, Laurie Chandler, Christy Plaice, Jenny Carter, and Tiffany Setzer: each of you has loved me well and created the safe space for my heart to birth this labor of love. You are treasures to me, and you make my life rich with laughter and love!

To Lisa Ham, God has gifted you with a heart of compassion as rich as your skillful eye for editorial and structural detail. From the smallest detail to the larger picture, your care for the structure of this book has allowed its content to shine. I am so grateful not only for your professionalism, but also for your beautiful spirit. Thank you.

To Yvonne Parks at PearCreative, what a joy to work with you, my sister in Dutch-ness! Your eye for clean design, your professionalism and promptness, and your gracious spirit have been a delight to experience. Thank you for bringing life so beautifully to this cover project. And of course, to Katherine Lloyd at The DESK, thank you for your enthusiasm, flexibility, and cheerful guidance throughout the publishing process. Your energy and expertise have been invaluable in moving this project through to completion! Thank you for being the experienced and capable guide that I very much needed.

Finally, to my clients, who over the years have courageously allowed me to guide you through the experience of IFS in therapy, I honor you and am so grateful for your journeys to Self-led living. What a deep and sacred honor to be entrusted with your hearts.

ABOUT THE AUTHOR

Jenna Riemersma is the founder and clinical director of the Atlanta Center for Relational Healing and is a teaching faculty member for the International Institute of Trauma and Addiction Professionals. She speaks widely, bringing the healing message of Internal Family Systems to audiences across the nation.

Jenna holds a master's degree in professional counseling from Richmont Graduate University. She is a Licensed Professional Counselor (LPC), an Internal Family Systems therapist (IFS), an EMDR-trained trauma therapist, a Certified Multiple Addiction Therapist Supervisor (CMAT-S, CSAT-S), and a National Certified Counselor (NCC).

She also holds a master's degree in public policy from Harvard University, and in her previous career she served in various legislative capacities on Capitol Hill.

Jenna has been happily married for twenty-five years and is the proud mom of two young adults and one golden retriever rescue. She is an animal lover and yoga enthusiast.

The Atlanta Center for Relational Healing
1640 Powers Ferry Road
Building 22, Suite 300
Marietta, GA 30067
404.981.2026
www.acfrh.com
www.jennariemersma.com

Made in United States
Orlando, FL
22 November 2022

24874948R00127